SAS AND ELITE FORCES GUIDE

ARMED COMBAT

SAS AND ELITE FORCES GUIDE
ARMED COMBAT

FIGHTING WITH WEAPONS IN EVERYDAY SITUATIONS

MARTIN J. DOUGHERTY

LYONS PRESS
Guilford, Connecticut
An imprint of Globe Pequot Press

Published by Amber Books Ltd (www.amberbooks.co.uk)

This Lyons Press edition first published in 2013

Lyons Press is an imprint of Globe Pequot Press.

Library of Congress Cataloging-in-Publication Data is available on file.

ISBN: 978-0-7627-8784-5

Project Editor: Michael Spilling
Design: MRM Graphics
Illustrations: Tony Randell

Printed in Italy

10 9 8 7 6 5 4 3 2 1

Photos on pages 28–29, 86–87, and 224–225
courtesy US Library of Congress.

CONTENTS

INTRODUCTION

We often hear that something is a 'dangerous weapon' but in truth that phrase is meaningless. A weapon is a weapon and nothing more. It can be used for good or ill, or not at all, but it needs a guiding intellect. In the hands of a pacifist, the most lethal implement is harmless. In the hands of a psychopath, a fairly innocuous object can kill. In the hands of a friend, a weapon is a source of reassurance. Similarly, anyone can kill with their bare hands or an improvised weapon if they try hard enough. It is us that make

Armed and Dangerous

This soldier is armed with a fully automatic carbine. As a backup he has a handgun and a knife, and probably a grenade or two as well. These are simply tools; what makes him dangerous – or not – is his willingness to use them and the choices he makes about when and how.

weapons dangerous, not the other way around.

Humans today occupy a position right at the top of the food chain, but it was not always so. The natural weapons available to humans are fairly puny, and we are neither spectacularly fast nor powerful. True, human beings are agile, but this is more useful as a defensive trait, allowing us to escape predators by climbing into places that they cannot go. As a species we are best suited to hunting small game and gathering fruit and vegetables. As such, we rightfully occupy a place in the middle of the food chain, prey for some creatures and preying on others.

What changed that status was tool use. As well as being agile, humans are clever, and our species learned to improvise and later craft tools to assist in survival. Of those tools, arguably the most important were those falling into the subset we call weapons – tools intended to cause harm to other living things.

Armed with spear, club and crude hatchet, a lone primitive human was a match for creatures that otherwise would kill and eat him. With a bow, and as part of a similarly armed party, our primitive ancestor elevated himself to the status of apex predator, capable of bringing down the largest of land creatures. Firearms simply tipped the odds further in our favour.

Improvised Weapons

Almost any object can be pressed into service as a weapon, but stabbing and puncturing implements are perhaps the easiest to use of all.

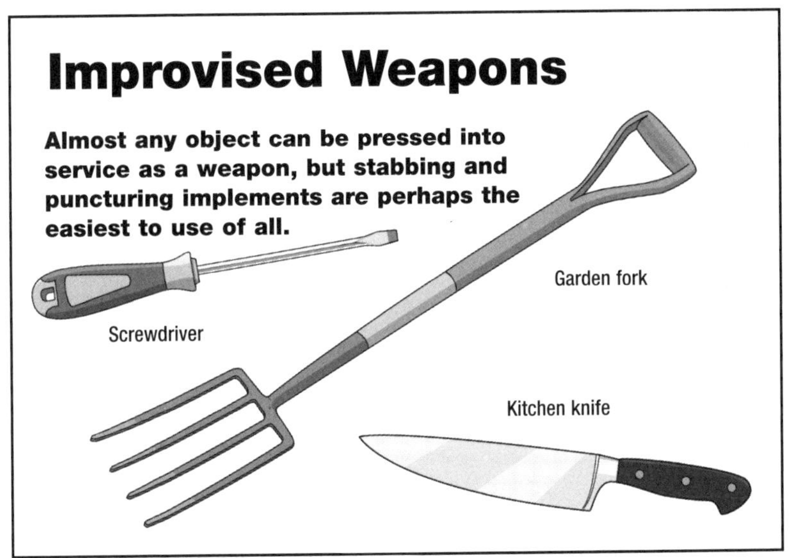

Thus it is today that armed humans are the most dangerous creatures inhabiting planet Earth, and this creates a situation where the most serious threat is not a sabre-tooth tiger or wolf pack, but another human.

The weapons that made us masters of our world also make us a threat to one another. Fortunately, the same tools can be used to defend and protect as to attack and destroy. Weapons are tools, and, like all tools, how they are used very much depends on the user.

Types of Weapon

There are essentially three types of hand weapon, sometimes categorized as 'Pointed, Sharp, Blunt' or 'PSB'. Each has its own unique characteristics, influencing how it is used or defended against.

Sharp Weapons

Sharp or bladed weapons come in two general types: those that have enough mass to hack deep into flesh; and those with lighter or smaller blades, which need to move along the surface in order to cut.

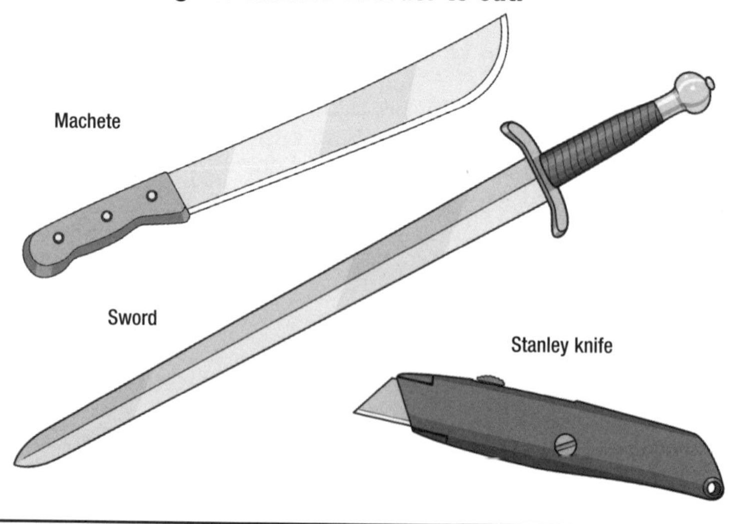

Pointed weapons include all stabbing implements such as the tip of a knife or sword, a screwdriver or anything that can be driven into a target. Pointed weapons are potentially the most lethal of all hand weapons as they cause deep wounds that can reach vital organs or cause massive internal bleeding. Pointed weapons can be pushed into the target with little effort and do not need a big swing to be effective. Conversely, they are only dangerous along a straight line from the tip. Anything off this line is not in danger until the weapon is redirected.

Sharp weapons have a cutting edge, and must move in contact with the target in order to be effective. Such weapons include knives and swords, as well as improvised sharp-edged weapons such as broken bottles. A sharp weapon that is held immobile cannot cut, but conversely a slashing action can make contact with flesh at any point and cause injury; it is easier to deflect a stab than a cut.

Blunt instruments rely on impact

Blunt Instruments

Blunt instruments are easy to obtain. The most dangerous of them concentrate force at the striking point by their shape. This is what makes a hammer capable of inflicting serious wounds.

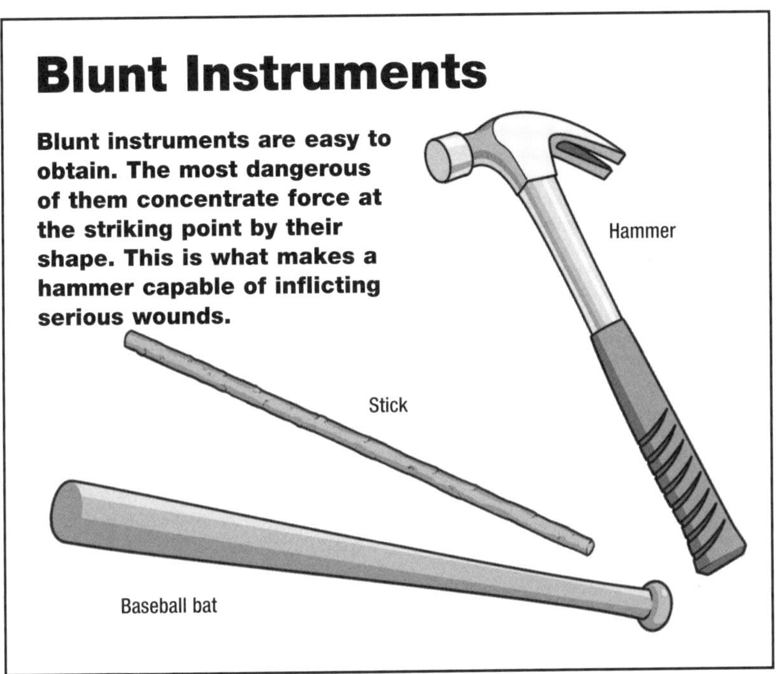

Telescopic Baton

Spring batons consist of sprung-steel sections contained within a metal handle. A flick of the wrist extends the baton, and it can be used to deliver stunning blows to joints or the side of the head.

to cause injury, using a combination of the weight and the force with which they are swung. A blunt weapon can be used to cause pain or force compliance by grinding it against a sensitive area of the body, such as a baton used to apply a restraint hold, but for the most part blunt weapons are swung (or sometimes thrust) to impact the target area, causing tissue trauma and breaking bones. An immobile blunt weapon, or one that there is little room to swing, is not a serious threat.

Some weapons are a combination of these factors. For example an axe uses impact to cause injury, but concentrates the force of its blow using a sharp edge. Others use the principles in other ways. Projectile weapons (i.e. firearms) cause a penetrating injury much like a pointed weapon, but do so by a combination of the mass and high velocity of the bullet. A firearm at close range can be used as a fairly reasonable club, but can best be thought of as an extremely long pointed weapon – anything on a line from the barrel to the nearest solid object is in severe danger if the trigger is pulled, but a gun that is pointed elsewhere can cause little harm unless it is redirected.

Stopping Power vs Lethality

We often hear of the lethality of weapons – their ability to cause the target to die – but this is actually a lesser consideration to the soldier, police officer or civilian facing a desperate threat. What matters is stopping power, not necessarily killing power. Stopping power is the ability to 'stop' a target, i.e. to make him cease whatever he is doing and

Sniper Team

A sniper team provides a good example of lethality versus stopping power. If the sniper shoots, it will be at fairly long range and the emphasis is normally on lethality. A target that can continue to act for a few moments is not normally a problem. If the security element must fire, the threat is close and must be stopped before the team can be endangered; killing the target is far less important than stopping him from shooting.

collapse. The concept is normally connected with firearms but can be applied to all weapons.

A target that is 'stopped' may or may not die, but in the immediate future he (or she) will not be able to

Using a Taser

Tasers deliver a paralyzing electrical shock that instantly incapacitates the attacker. The operating switch on the device can be applied to deliver subsequent shocks.

act against the weapon's user or any other intended victim. For the soldier in combat, the lone police officer facing multiple assailants or the civilian under attack, this is what matters. An enemy who is out of the fight is out of the fight whether he dies then and there (or later) or makes a full recovery. An enemy who can continue to shoot or fight for a time, even if he will collapse and die eventually, is still a threat until he goes down.

Thus when choosing a weapon for close-range combat, military personnel and law enforcement officers prefer a weapon that will 'put down' an opponent over one that is more likely to kill, but not straight away. An assassin or a sniper might choose lethality over stopping power, but those who fight primarily at close range want the opponent downed or disabled and incapable of fighting on – anything else comes a long way second.

As a general rule, pointed weapons and firearms are the most likely to kill of all weapon types, with blunt instruments the least likely and blades somewhere in between. However, it is possible to kill with any weapon, whether this is intended or not. For this reason, knives are not ideal for civilian self-defence. It is very easy to kill someone outright with a knife, even if the intent was only to injure or frighten, and not all knife wounds kill straight away. Thus a knife suffers from the twin problems of being perhaps too lethal and not quick enough to disable an opponent. For self-defence, a blunt instrument is more likely to cause incapacitating injury without being lethal.

For soldiers in combat, this consideration is not as critical – the aim is to win the fight by whatever means, and killing the enemy is an integral part of warfare. A knife is an ideal tool for what amounts to assassination, such as taking out an enemy sentry quickly and quietly. It also makes a good, versatile fighting tool with many other applications, and is easy to carry. For this reason a knife is an essential part of a soldier's kit, but a police officer will normally carry a baton for situations where less lethality is desirable.

Generally speaking, a skilled and determined fighter armed with any weapon (or even none) is likely to be more effective than a frightened or half-hearted person equipped with an excellent weapon. Having said that, a weapon is a great 'force-multiplier', enabling the puny human to take on dangerous animals or a single skilled fighter to take down a series of less effective opponents. All else being equal, any weapon is better than no weapon.

Legality of Weapon Use

For police officers and military personnel, there are clear guidelines about when weapons can be used.

Searching for Hidden Weapons

Most people who carry weapons with the intent to use them (as opposed to trying to smuggle them into a secured area such as an airport) carry them in accessible locations that are easily and quickly searched. A more detailed 'pat down' is necessary to reveal well-concealed items.

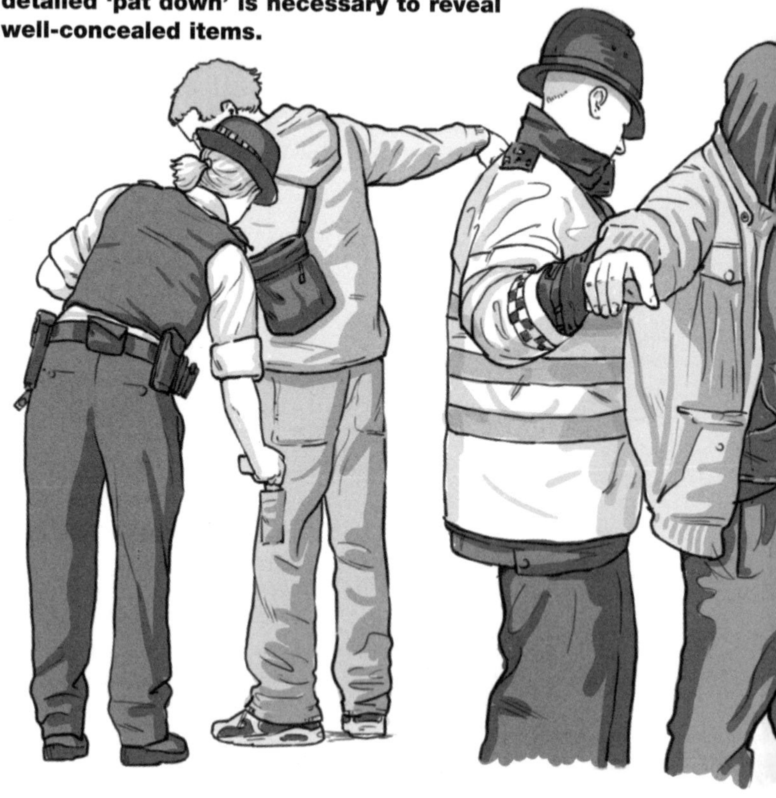

Security Expert Tip: Know How to Use It

Some people obtain weapons for self-protection or home defence, but benefit primarily from a placebo effect – i.e., they feel safer because they have a gun in a drawer or their bag. Carrying a weapon that you do not know how to deploy and use effectively makes you a liability to yourself and everyone around. If you obtain a weapon, get trained with it.

Law enforcement officers work with a threat/response model whereby lethal force is only used where absolutely necessary, such as when an officer perceives a clear threat to someone's life or safety. This means that there are circumstances where it might be legal to use a baton but not a handgun.

Much the same comments apply to military personnel engaged in security operations, but for troops operating in a war zone the response is more all-or-nothing. Enemy combatants can be engaged with any weapon that has been issued; noncombatants cannot. Some hostiles muddy the waters by hiding among and dressing like the civilian population, so the question can become one of correctly identifying enemy targets. Once identified, they can be engaged as necessary.

For civilians, the legalities of armed response more closely resemble those for police/security personnel than soldiers in a war zone. Response must be appropriate and proportionate to the threat and the circumstances. Under most conditions it is illegal to harm someone or even to threaten to do so, but when acting in self-defence a civilian is permitted to use necessary measures to ensure their own safety and that of others. This may include the use of a weapon.

Severe Threat

Laws vary from one place to another, but as a rule a person who is facing a severe threat will not be prosecuted for using a weapon. What matters is the severity of that threat and the level of force used to nullify it, and this is a matter of general threat level, not like-for-like.

For example, using a firearm against a knife-wielding attacker would generally be considered acceptable as both are lethal implements. There is no requirement to put aside the gun and find a knife of your own to ensure a fair fight.

Bodyguard Tip: Train Your Loved Ones

It can be worth looking at your situation as regards family and friends as if you were their bodyguard. The last thing you need is people you are trying to protect panicking or even rounding on you to give you a telling-off for being paranoid, violent or whatever. Brief your family and friends on what you might do in a dangerous situation, and how they can help you. This is most likely by getting themselves out of danger and calling for help.

Unarmed Threat

Once a confrontation or fight starts, instinctive behaviour is to use your hands to attack and defend. Someone who passes up an opportunity to strike in order to reach into a pocket is almost certainly going for a weapon.

Concealment and Deception

The aggressor has used deception (asking the time) to distract his target while he deploys a knife from a concealed location. Although very simple, tricks of this sort can be extremely effective.

Law Enforcement Tip: Know Where Your Gear Is

If you carry a weapon or have one stashed for home defence, make sure it is always in the same place. There is no time to scrabble through your sock drawer for the .45 you're sure is in there somewhere, or to grab for the place where you used to carry your weapon. If you own or carry a weapon, rehearse deploying it and if you change its position, retrain yourself to get to it quickly.

Normally, using a weapon against an unarmed attacker is likely to be considered excessive force; however, much depends upon the circumstances. A frail, elderly person who uses a gun or a knife to deal with an attacker who could otherwise easily overpower them is not likely to face prosecution; what other options were available?

Perceived Threat

Perception is also a key factor. A homeowner who sees an object in a midnight intruder's hand and shoots, or hits him with a heavy object, can argue that his use of the weapon was justified by the fact that he saw what he believed to be a weapon. If it turns out to be something harmless then the homeowner is not necessarily transformed into a psychopath who shot or maimed an unarmed man... he used what seemed like a proportionate response to the situation as he perceived it.

To put that another way: if you genuinely believe that circumstances exist whereby an armed response is justified, then using a weapon is probably legal. For example, if police see someone brandishing a handgun and looking like he is about to shoot, they are not required to wait until he actually kills someone before they can open fire. They are legally entitled to act on their perception of the situation, and their actions will be judged on that perception. If the weapon turns out later to be a harmless replica, the shooting would still be justified.

Extreme Threat

Tackling a firearm user whilst unarmed is extremely dangerous and should only be done if you have nothing to lose – if you believe you are about to be killed, then anything you do is better than passively waiting for it to happen.

As an aside, this means that it is obviously not a good idea to run around the streets with imitation swords, knives or firearms. Anyone who does so (and who survives the response) has no justification for complaints of excessive force if and when they are confronted by armed police officers. If you have what looks like a weapon and you act like it is a real one, then you can expect others to react as if it is, too.

Certain actions can make it seem as if an individual is armed and reaching for a weapon. People involved in a confrontation instinctively keep their hands between them and the opponent, or wave them around in what is known as posturing, trying to exert dominance. A hand that disappears under clothing or into a bag during a confrontation is almost certainly coming back with a weapon. The time to deal with this is before the weapon is deployed; once it is in action, a response might be too late.

Our hands are our main weapons, and it is instinctive to keep them more or less between us and a threat during any confrontation. Some people will splay their hands in order to look bigger and more intimidating, but nobody sticks their hands in their pockets whilst involved in a heated argument, unless they want something that is in the pocket. If hands come up, especially with clenched fists, then an attack is imminent but at least it will not be with a weapon. Hands that disappear under clothing are a sign that something much more serious is about to unfold.

Police officers and security professionals are taught to watch for

Special Forces Tip: Use It Or Lose It!

If someone brings a weapon into a situation, they create a potentially lethal scenario, in which they are likely to have to use the weapon or be disarmed and have it turned on them. The time to consider whether or not you are willing to use a weapon against another human being is long before an armed confrontation develops.

Trainers' Tip: Be Prepared, Not Paranoid

There is no need to be a paranoid lunatic and assume that hordes of assailants are waiting around every corner. Most people do not encounter armed violence in their lives, so preparation is a matter of 'just in case'. For those who go in harm's way as part of their job, a higher level of training makes sense because the risk is greater. If preparing to defend your life is taking up so much of it that it's not worth living, then you're overdoing it.

'tells' that someone might be carrying a weapon and will react if they are suspicious. Normally this is by means of situation control techniques – physical repositioning, clear, spoken commands and possibly the deployment of a weapon as a broad hint to desist. However, someone who looks like they are drawing a weapon on a police officer can expect to be shot, hit with a baton or otherwise robustly dealt with. Other weapon users will react similarly, and with less restraint, so it is a generally good idea to keep things calm and make sure that the person you are arguing with can see that you are not reaching for a weapon.

In many areas it is quite legal to carry a weapon for self-defence or have one in the home for the same purposes. If it is not, then carrying a weapon is a criminal offence. This can create the odd situation where actually using a weapon might be justifed in self-defence, but having it in the first place was not and so a prosecution may occur.

In Britain, for example, it is illegal to carry any object for the purposes of using it as a weapon, even if that object would be legal if used for its normal purposes. So a plumber who has a large wrench on the car seat beside him might face some hard questions if stopped by the police. The same wrench in a toolbox in the back seat along with other tools of the trade would be perfectly legal. Under British law it is acceptable to

Weapon Transportation and the Law

I own a lot of swords, and carry them around from place to place. They travel in a big zipped-up bag with 'fencing' written on the side, along with masks, gloves, jackets and other paraphernalia associated with historical fencing. If challenged about the weapons, I have a good reason to be carrying them – these are fencing weapons and I'm going to a fencing class or coming home from one. All the other fencing-related stuff makes this seem quite plausible, so the answer would probably be accepted at face value.

If I were to run down the street waving one of my swords at people, I could (and should) be arrested. The weapons

A rifle carried in a proper bag is a lot less threatening than one openly carried in your hands.

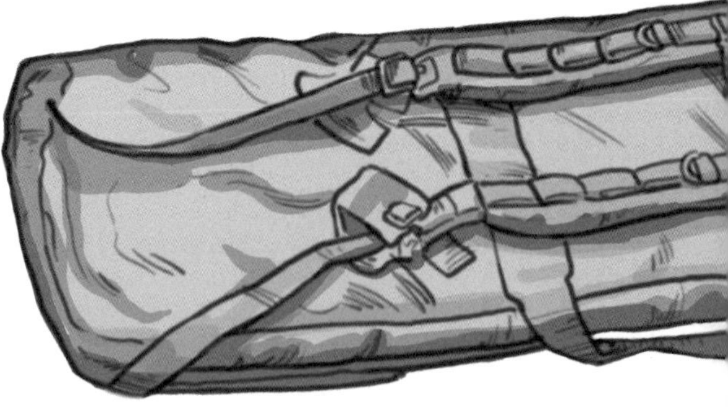

are actually designed to be safe to fence with; we hit one another with them on a regular basis. However, they look real and could cause harm if swung hard enough. Someone seeing one being brandished would have cause to believe it was a serious threat, and this might justify an armed response.

In other words, common sense needs to be applied to transporting any weapon. Waving what looks like a real sword in a threatening manner could get me shot, and the person doing the shooting would probably not be prosecuted, yet carrying them in the bag is quite legal.

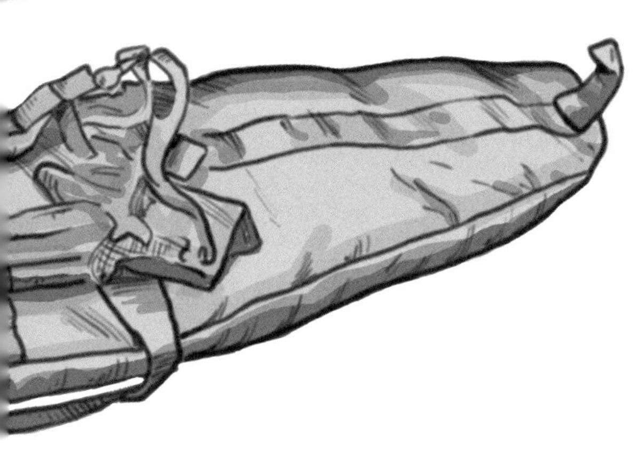

Legitimate Use of Weapons

If you use a weapon that you are legally permitted to have, then the only question is whether the use of that weapon constitutes reasonable force under self-defence law. However, weapons are forbidden by law in some localities. Taking a weapon into such an area 'just in case' would not be lawful and you might be prosecuted, even in circumstances where you were justified in using the weapon. If, on the other hand, a confrontation turned nasty and you used a weapon that happened to be there (perhaps a kitchen knife or a tool that was present for a legitimate purpose), this would be an entirely different situation in law from going armed into a confrontation you could have avoided. If violence is brought to you and you have no choice but to defend yourself, arming yourself may well be justified, even if weapons are not normally allowed in that locality.

grab an object for use as a weapon if the threat necessitates it, though it may be necessary to explain why the object was present in the first place.

Someone who grabs a knife from the kitchen to deal with an armed intruder, or a group of intruders who seem intent on serious harm, has a pretty solid explanation for why the weapon was there, and the circumstances seem to necessitate it. Similarly, our plumber might be justified in grabbing his wrench from the toolbox in order to stop a gang from carjacking him; the object was there for an innocent purpose, but circumstances indicated that a weapon was necessary.

In localities were weapon carry is legal, the situation is simpler. There is no need to justify why the weapon was present if it is legal to have it, but of course its deployment and use must still be necessitated by the circumstances.

As a general rule, if you could not avoid the situation or withdraw from it safely, and the only way to effectively protect yourself or others was to use a weapon (or threaten its use), then that would be considered a legal use of force.

Hidden Knife

A small knife is easy to conceal in the hand and remains ready for instant use. A good rule is that if you cannot see the palms of someone's hands, you have reason to suspect they may be holding a weapon.

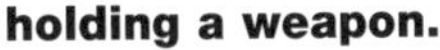

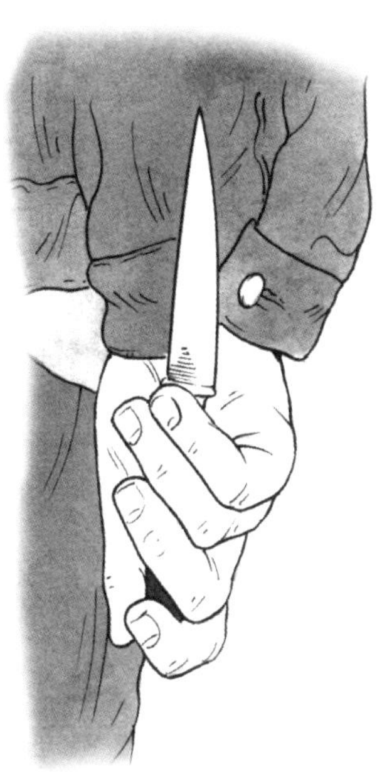

Effective use of a weapon is dependent on the mindset behind it. Control, timing and focus are essential to succeeding in combat – the fighter who masters his fear, picks his moment with care and strikes with both precision and intent will walk away alive. This mindset, combined with a solid understanding of how to use a given weapon, is invaluable to the soldier or law-enforcement officer.

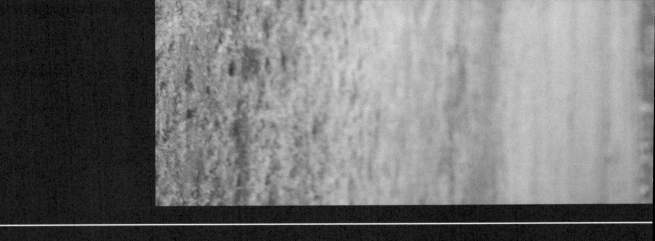

PART ONE: THE ESSENCE OF ARMED COMBAT

1

Fighting Skills and Mindset

Combat of any sort is frightening and often painful, even for the victor.

Regardless of the weapons involved, victory often goes to the side that is most motivated, best trained or simply the most willing to fight on when things are going badly. Fighting spirit and aggression count for at least as much as weapons-handling skill.

Making an attack with a weapon is always a risk. If the opponent avoids or blocks the strike, the attacker is more vulnerable to a counterattack than if he had remained 'on guard' to protect himself. Indeed, there are some circumstances (such as an armed fighter vs an unarmed one) where the would-be attacker is more or less invulnerable until he commits to striking a blow. However, standing around ready to defend is not a route to victory either.

Picking the Moment

Winning a fight with weapons is a matter of picking the right moment to attack, and using timing and control of distance to land a telling blow without being hit in return. Most attacks are simple, direct and brutal. There is little of the subtlety found in sports such as boxing or fencing, where athletes try to trick one another into making a mistake using

Weapons trainers spend as much effort on 'combative mindset' as they do on actual weapon-handling skills.

Fence Position

Something as simple as keeping your hands in between you and an aggressive person can deter an attack by making them keep their distance. This is known as a 'fence position' and is not aggressive or threatening, but helps keep control of a situation.

subtle feints or clever combination attacks. More commonly, an armed opponent will rush in and strike when he thinks the moment is right. If he succeeds, the matter may be over instantly. If not, his opponent may be able to successfully counterattack. There are essentially three ways to defeat an armed attack:

- Intercept the attacker
- Evade the attack
- Block or deflect the attack.

Interception is a matter of hitting the opponent before he can land his blow. This can be a risky technique, though sometimes it is the best option. For example, a soldier or

Law Enforcement Tip: Confidence and Resolution

Combat is frightening, even for trained personnel. It is necessary to maintain the resolve to fight through and win, even when the odds are poor. Confidence in your skills, training, comrades and weaponry are vital to maintaining this resolve.

police officer armed with a handgun can shoot an onrushing knife-armed attacker before he gets close enough to strike. This is where stopping power is of paramount importance; if the attacker falls dead after stabbing his target, then the interception has, to all intents and purposes, failed. The same applies to most hand weapons; if the attacker runs right on to the point of a soldier's knife but is still able to cause injury or death, then interception was the wrong choice.

Evading a Blow

Simply ducking under a swing may ensure it does not land, but it is better to use the evasion to close in and launch an effective counterattack. This soldier has moved forward and to the side, and is now well positioned to demolish the attacker.

Evading the attack is a matter of moving so that it does not land. One option is to sidestep or move back so that the attack falls short, or to duck under a wild swing. The drawback with evasion is that it does nothing to stop the opponent from simply making another attack.

However, evasion can be combined with an interception. For example, a soldier might sidestep a bayonet attack and shoot the attacker, or duck a swing with an entrenching tool while stabbing with his knife. This turns the evasion into an offensive-defence that has a good chance of putting the opponent out of the fight. The opponent has closed the distance and made himself vulnerable to a counterattack; the defender evades to protect himself while taking advantage of the opportunity to land a return blow.

Blocking is a matter of putting something in the way to stop an attack. Usually this is a weapon, but sometimes an object can be used defensively as a shield. A block takes the force of the opponent's attack, whereas deflecting the attack is more subtle. The attack is knocked aside rather than being stopped cold. Generally speaking, stabs are easier

Deflection Defence

Attacks that are coming straight in, such as a knife thrust, can be deflected to the side with a sweeping motion. This combines deflection with an element of evasion.

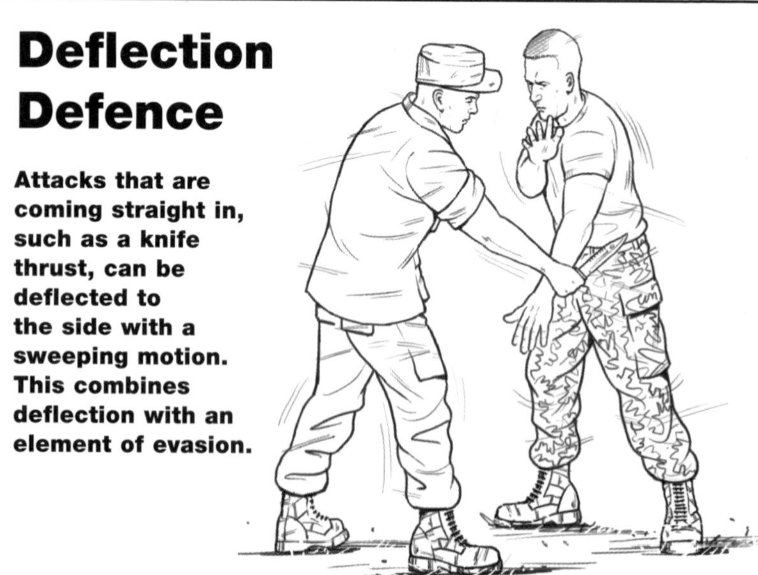

to deflect than cuts or swings. Often, a combination of these methods is used. For example, a soldier might sidestep a bayonet thrust and at the same time push it aside with a sweeping motion of his arm, giving him a double chance of defeating the attack. A police officer might step back out of reach as an knifeman thrusts at him, striking the extended knife arm with his baton to combine interception and deflection.

There are other options in the face of an armed attack. One is to get behind something solid, i.e. to take cover. This is the only good option in the face of a firearm unless the defender is close enough to grab it or can shoot first. Cover can be used against hand weapons, but as a rule someone close enough to attack with a hand-held weapon will be able to climb over cover or run around it, so at best the obstacle gains the defender time for a counterattack.

Body Armour

The final option is to hope that body armour stops an attack or that any injury inflicted is not too serious. Sometimes there is no better option than to take a knife slash on the arm in order to protect the neck; if this permits the defender to get

Body Armour

Body armour such as the system seen here will protect the wearer from all manner of ballistic threats, including rifle-calibre firearms. Its drawback is its bulk and weight, which can make moving exhausting.

a fight-ending blow in, he should then be able to obtain medical attention and will have won – albeit at a price. Accepting a knife attack to the body in the hope that a stab vest will function correctly is not a combat technique that police officers are taught (with good reason), but it may be that there is absolutely no alternative. If the officer emerges alive and victorious from the fight, then the gambit has worked.

This is the essence of armed combat: combatants must be willing to do whatever it takes to win. That may mean fighting on with serious injuries, or taking a hair-raising gamble to land that fight-winning blow. However, for the most part a cool head and a sensible tradeoff of risk to potential gain, coupled with skilled weapons handling, will result in good odds of victory. Nothing is ever guaranteed, but as a rule the fighter who keeps his fear under control, picks his moment carefully and strikes with both precision and intent will walk away alive.

Picking Your Fights

Military forces are sometimes required to deal with unexpected attacks, or to launch an operation with inadequate preparation because a situation requires it. However, this is not a recipe that guarantees success. Military commanders prefer to pick their fights and to stack the odds before combat begins. The best weapons, training and tactics are brought to bear where the enemy is weak, inadequately trained or poorly equipped.

The same applies to small-scale armed combat. It is possible to virtually ensure victory by stacking the odds. Attacking by surprise (or concealing the weapon until it is time to strike), in overwhelming force or with greater skill increases the chances of success. Possessing superior weapons, or any weapon where the opponent has none, is also a huge advantage. Having a weapon is also a potent psychological factor.

Regardless of the relative merits of any given weapon system, holding a weapon tends to make a fighter more confident and willing to engage in combat. Thus it is wise to assume that anyone brandishing a weapon is willing to use it. Tackling an armed opponent is highly risky at the best of times, and if there is another solution then it may be the best course of action. Special Forces troops attempt to accomplish their missions wherever possible without contact with the enemy, making it unnecessary to engage in armed combat. When they do have to confront the enemy, they try not to give him much chance to use his

Special Forces Tip: Short Fights are Good Fights

As a general rule, a short fight is better than a long one. If the opposition can be taken out quickly, there will be less friendly casualties and less chance for the enemy to receive assistance or to escape.

weapon, taking enemy personnel out of the fight before they can start shooting. Anything resembling a fair fight is highly undesirable.

The same applies to the civilian who finds himself facing a weapon. Ideally, if there is any suspicion that a weapon may be present then conflict should be avoided, perhaps by leaving the area. If it is necessary to tackle a weapon, or a suspected weapon, then the time to do so is before the user has deployed it. If someone starts to draw a knife or gun during a confrontation, the odds will only get worse once he has done so. An all-out attack can take him out of the fight before he has deployed his weapon.

Only in the most desperate situation would anyone – military or

Restraining an Assailant

'Control and restraint' techniques are the province of police and security personnel, who can use handcuffs to ensure that a restrained opponent stays that way. There is no point in using restraint methods unless they can bring the situation to a satisfactory conclusion.

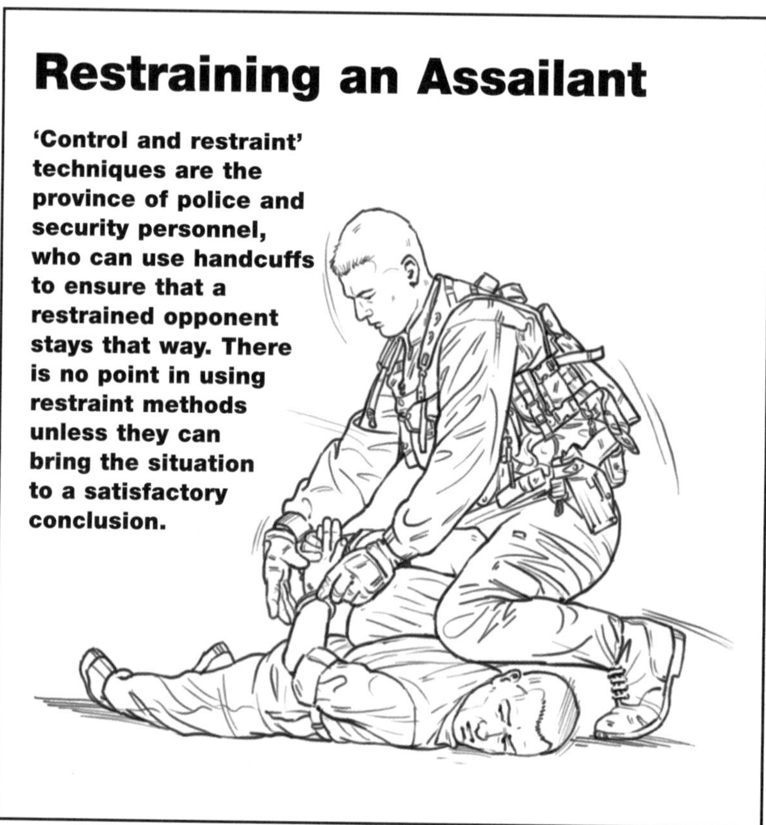

otherwise – take on an armed opponent with no weapon of his own. Sometimes a weapon can be grabbed or improvised, which can even the odds. In a war zone, or for a police officer facing an armed suspect, there is little need to worry about legalities of weapons use at this point. So long as excessive force is not used (e.g. stabbing/beating a detained prisoner or suspect) then the soldier or officer is only doing his duty. However, some civilians may hesitate to arm themselves or act against an armed threat due to fear of the law.

The law varies from one place to another, but as a general rule anyone facing an armed attack is justified in doing whatever is necessary to stop it. Grabbing a weapon, even a potentially lethal implement such as knife, should be justifiable in the face of armed attack; the defender should worry about not getting killed rather than whether or not it would be lawful to use a weapon.

Once the attack is stopped, then much the same 'rules of engagement' apply to military personnel, law-enforcement officers and civilians – it is not normally lawful to use a weapon against a surrendered or incapacitated hostile. And there is usually no need, as a 'stopped' assailant is no longer a threat.

The simple rule for armed threats is to avoid them wherever possible, escape from or evade them if you can, and if it proves necessary then do whatever you must to win.

Essential Skills

Many weapons – especially firearms – are virtually useless in the hands of someone who does not know how to use them. In close-quarters combat, fiddling with a safety catch or struggling to reload an awkward weapon can cost the user his life. Some hand-to-hand weapons are also very difficult to use. For example, some of the more esoteric martial arts weapons are as much a danger to the unskilled user as to the opponent. Someone who picks up a set of nunchaku or a three-section staff for the first time is as likely to injure himself as anyone else.

Even apparently simple weapons can be deceptively hard to use, and attempting to employ an unfamiliar weapon can actually make a fighter less effective. Thus weapon-handling skills are essential to armed combat, although the degree of skill necessary varies depending upon the calibre of the threat. For example, almost anyone can pick up a stick or knife and defeat an unarmed and not very skilled opponent, but a trained soldier or martial artist might well be able to simply take the weapon away or beat the user senseless despite it.

The degree of skill required to win a given fight depends on what the opposition is armed with and how skilled he is. By way of illustration, it requires relatively little unarmed combat training to be able to deal with a drunk civilian throwing wild punches outside a pizza shop at 2.00 AM, but a highly skilled mixed martial arts fighter is a different prospect. So it is with armed combat; anyone can swing a stick at an opponent, but a skilled stick fighter will effortlessly demolish an untrained opponent.

Weapon Mechanics

Thus the most basic requirement to be able to fight effectively with any given weapon is an understanding of how that weapon works, i.e. the mechanics of causing injury with it. The user must know how and where to strike, and must understand any enabling factors such as posture and footwork.

One common mistake is to underestimate the momentum of a weapon and either not be able to get it moving fast enough – which leads to missing opportunities to land a blow or, worse, to block one – or over-extending on a failed attack (which leaves the user open to a counter strike).

The weapon user must also understand related concepts such as timing and distance. Knowing how far he can reach with the weapon without overextending allows the user to strike at enemies who may think they are safely out of reach, and to avoid becoming vulnerable by over-extending. Timing is also of critical importance – knowing instinctively how long a weapon will take to reach its target at any given distance allows the user to strike at just the right time, catching the opponent as he moves in to attack or when he is otherwise vulnerable.

The more skilled a user is with any given weapon, the more he will come to understand concepts such as 'lines of attack'. The body mechanics associated with any given weapon

Special Forces Tip: Controlled Aggression

Controlled aggression wins fights. Nervous defence generally does not. It is pointless to blindly charge in, but once combat begins a force that is fighting to win has a huge advantage over one that is merely trying not to lose.

Get Behind the Knife

One common technique for dealing with armed attacks is to move so that the weapon is pointed away from you. In this case, the soldier has stepped around so that he is 'behind' the knife, ensuring that it cannot be thrust into his body.

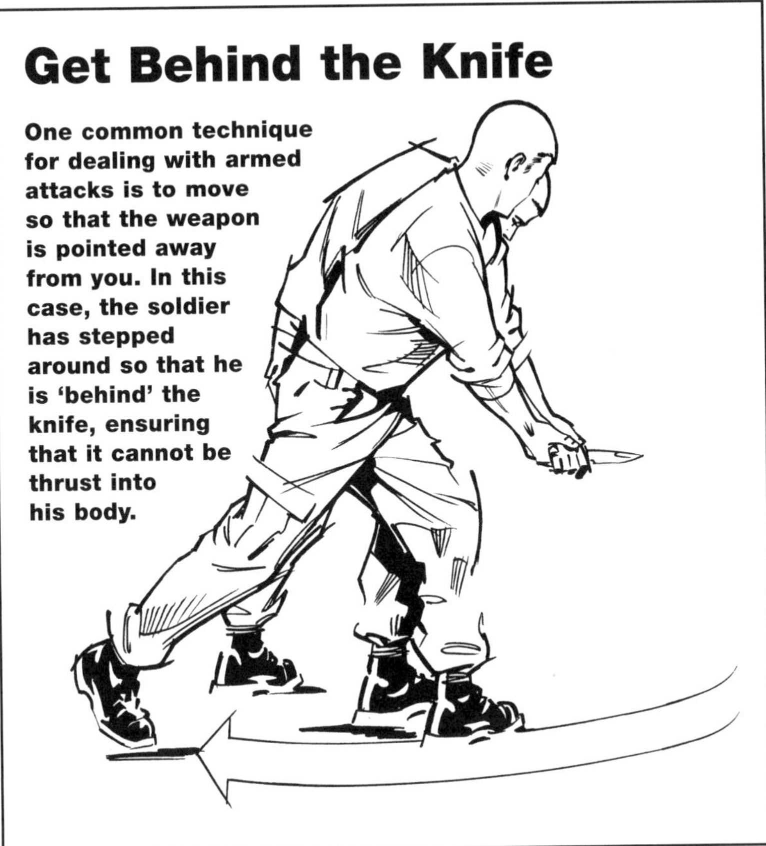

cause it to move most easily along certain paths. Cross-referencing this with a knowledge of the likely targets allows the fighter to predict where an opponent is likely to attack, and even when.

For example, a stick or baton is a blunt weapon and must normally be swung to cause harm. A skilled user might do something clever like thrusting it at the opponent's face, but most people armed with a stick will not think of doing this.

A soldier or police officer armed with a baton, facing an assailant armed with a stick or similar weapon, can make certain predictions. He cannot be certain that the opponent

A
B

Three-foot Stick versus Bayonet

The defender first evades and deflects the bayonet thrust using the stick (A), then strikes to the throat with his forearm (B), which sends the end of the stick over the opponent's shoulder. Forearm and stick apply a choke to the opponent as he is pulled in tight (C). When he collapses, the soldier disengages and retrieves the stick.

Knife Fight

The attacker takes the initiative with a forehand slash aimed at the neck (2) and immediately follows the movement with a cut to the abdomen (3). Neither is guaranteed to stop the opponent immediately, so the attacker follows up by grabbing the opponent and dragging him onto a stab to the chest (4).

will not do something clever or unorthodox, but he can figure out the likely threats.

Anticipating an Attack

The opponent is holding his weapon in his right hand, at the right side of his body. If he wants to make a backhand attack, he will have to move his weapon hand across the body, and the defender will see this. The distance between the fighters is such that an attack to the body or legs will require the opponent to close in, which again the defender will spot and possibly intercept. So it follows that the most likely attack is a forehand swing at the head, probably diagonally downward. An unskilled combatant might not see that coming; to a trained fighter it is obvious. Even a modest amount of training allows the soldier or police officer to recognize where the attack is coming from, and his experience should also allow him to 'read' the opponent's intentions. For example, someone who holds a knife close to their body is confident with it and will probably be willing to close in and make a lethal attack.

Someone who holds the knife at arm's length is actually using it as a sort of shield and may not be willing to attack at all. There are never any guarantees, of course, but the way the opponent holds his weapon often indicates whether he wants to use it or not, and what he is planning to do.

Threatening Intention

Someone who shows a weapon normally wants something and is using the weapon to get it. This does not mean that he will not use it, but this is not usually the primary intention.

Guiding Intent

As already noted, a weapon is no use without a guiding intent. Most civilians who use weapons do so because they are forced to, or out of fear. A mugger may intend only to frighten the victim with his weapon by waving it around, but could instinctively stab or slash if he is attacked. There have been countless tragedies where someone has intended only to use a knife as a threat, perhaps carrying it only because they were frightened of being attacked, but ended up using it.

There are two main reasons for this to happen. The first is that a weapon tends to give its user confidence. So a person who would normally avoid conflict chooses to seek a confrontation, comforted by the knife in their pocket. When this leads to a fight, they use the weapon to survive and may end up in jail.

Alternatively, sometimes the threat of a weapon is not credible. When the 'victim' suddenly produces a weapon, a potential assailant might be deterred – but only if he thinks the weapon will be used, and used effectively. If he thinks the victim will not use his weapon, or that he can win anyway, then he may well choose to attack. At this point the weapon user has a stark choice to make – to use his weapon and accept the consequences, or possibly have it used against him. There are some

Finishing Moves

A 'knee drop' can be used to finish a downed opponent by breaking his ribs. Even if this is not achieved, the attack is extremely painful and may wind the opponent, while weight on the knee will immobilize him.

simple rules for weapons carry:

- Do not carry any weapon unless you are willing and able to use it, and to accept the consequences of doing so.
- Do not deploy a weapon unless you are prepared to use it.
- If you deploy a weapon as a threat, you must be prepared to use it, and the opponent must be able to recognize this.

These concepts are built into military and law enforcement weapons-use training. Personnel are not sent out with weapons they are unable or unwilling to use, and in many cases this means that they may not have to. When a uniformed police officer or base security guard aims a weapon at someone, there is usually an assumption that he or she is willing to shoot. That may force surrender or compliance with an arrest and render actual use of the weapon unnecessary.

Most importantly, having brought a weapon into the equation, the user absolutely must be willing to use it. If not, he is gambling on the threat being enough to deter the opponent. If it is not, the weapon user will likely be killed… quite possibly with his own weapon.

Combative Mindset

A combative mindset is a part of military and law enforcement training. It is every bit as vital as fighting skills – perhaps even more so. It is possible to win a fight without skill, but without a willingness to fight through to the end, defeat is certain. A properly trained weapons user understands the risks inherent in engaging in combat, but has the confidence and courage to accept them in return for the prospect of victory.

A typical person, confronted with an armed assailant, might subconsciously ask 'what is he going to do to me?', but someone with the correct combative mindset is more likely to ask, 'how best do I stop him?'. Similarly, there are those who will quail in fear upon seeing a weapon, and those who think 'I want that' and set about obtaining it.

Many people are unwilling to strike a blow or fire a shot, not least because they know they are about to hurt someone. Those under the influence of drugs or alcohol, or who are extremely angry are more likely to simply use the weapon and worry about consequences later, if ever. This means that the 'bad guys' are more willing to use weapons than decent people, which is not a good thing for civilized society.

However, those that protect society – police, soldiers and good citizens in a bad situation – can develop a mindset that allows them to do what is necessary without hesitation, and they can do it without turning into bad people.

Trainer's Tip: Fear and Cowardice

Fear is not the same thing as cowardice. Cowardice is defined as the inability to overcome fear in order to do what must be done, while fear is a natural reaction to dangerous circumstances and is felt by most people to some degree or other. Good training and high levels of confidence can result in one person not really being frightened while another is terrified, but neither is a coward nor necessarily a hero.

State of Mind

A combative mindset is nothing to do with being a psychopath or gaining enjoyment from hurting others. It is simply a state of mind where necessity pushes aside hesitation. This is also important when dealing with the aftermath of an incident; someone who knows that they did only what they had to is less likely to suffer from mental health issues than an individual who spends years afterwards asking if they should have struck that blow or fired the shot.

Thus the combative mindset, developed in training, permits the soldier or law-enforcement officer to deal with the situation at hand by fighting effectively, and to cope with emotional trauma afterwards. This is vital, since weapons use often takes just a few seconds; but those seconds can be life changing. A bad decision can result in death or permanent injury, or years of mental torture replaying an incident and wondering what could have been done differently.

A combative mindset is also important when a combatant is hit or wounded. Many injuries received, even from firearms, will not 'stop' a determined fighter and may not be life-threatening. Yet the majority of people will fold up around a wound in panic. There are times when the only possible course of action is to get pressure on the wound and hope help arrives fast, but if there are hostiles still in the fight then someone who is trying to deal with an injury becomes an easy target.

Coping with Injury

In order to win, it is often necessary to fight on with an injury and seek medical attention afterwards.

A combative mindset is essential in this case. A soldier who knows he has been shot or stabbed, but realizes that the wound cannot be too serious because he is still able to fight, can struggle on and win. Sometimes this is the only way to survive.

Much depends on the fighter's state of mind. Someone who is non-fatally shot while in the middle of eating lunch will normally react defensively, covering the wound and falling to the ground. The same person, shot in the middle of charging at an enemy with his bayonet raised, may well continue his attack. This can be counterproductive; soldiers have died of their injuries because they fought on when it was not necessary, but when outnumbered and surrounded it is the only way to survive.

This mindset can be summed up as: 'It's not over until you give up or they kill you, and you're not dead.'

Bayonet Training

One way the military fosters a combative mindset is bayonet

Bayonet Fighting

A bayonet, like all thrusting weapons, is dangerous along a narrow path. If the defender can move off that path or deflect the weapon to the side, he will be safe until the attacker recovers his weapon and thrusts again.

training. Military personnel make use of the bayonet on very few occasions, yet bayonet training remains a part of military life. One reason for this is practical – it may actually be useful some day – but bayonet training also helps soldiers develop the necessary aggressive spirit and mindset. It is a hard thing to make the decision to rush forward and plunge a sharp implement into someone's body, but if it proves necessary then the more familiar the soldier is with the situation, the more likely he is to simply act when he needs to.

Bayonet Thrust

To make an effective thrust, the soldier first steps forward. This not only moves him into range but also puts moving body weight behind the thrust. From a firm base the soldier lunges his weapon out at the opponent before recovering to a well-balanced posture, ready to defend or attack again.

Much the same comments apply to martial sports in the military. The world's elite forces are highly unlikely to fence, box, wrestle or engage in a Brazilian jiu-jitsu match with their opponents on the battlefield, but these sports enable soldiers to face a combative challenge in a relatively safe environment, learning to deal with the stress of combat and – importantly – experiencing victory. Winning is a habit, and those who have experienced it get to like it.

In situations where the second-place prize is a military funeral, winning is a good habit to cultivate.

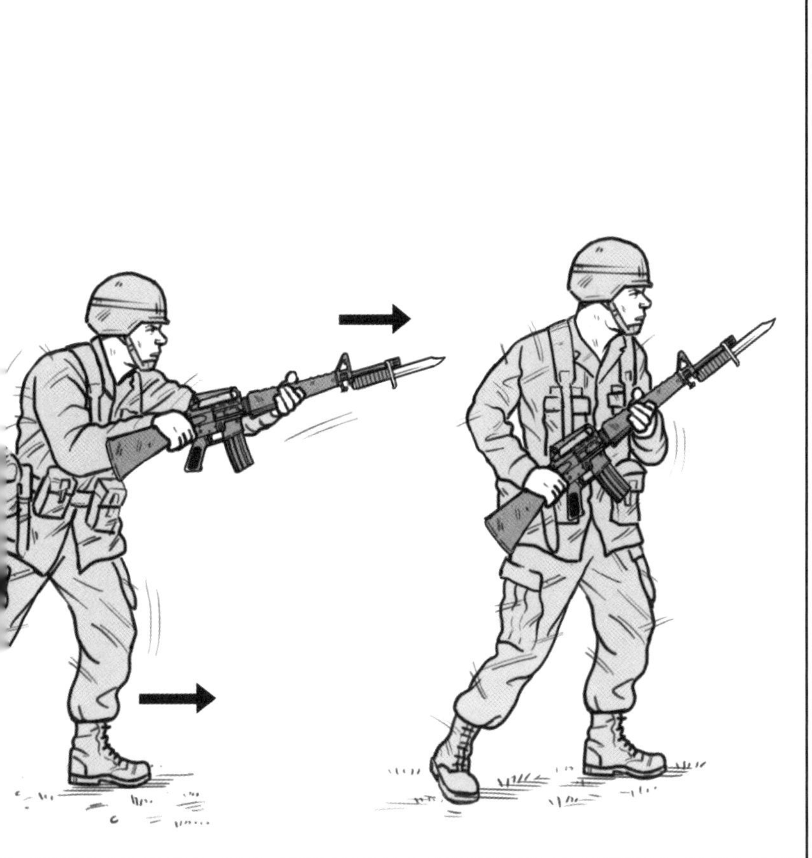

Parry with a Bayonet

The defender meets the thrust with a sideways hooking action, which does more than simply deflect the attack; it twists the opponent off balance and points his bayonet in a direction that does not threaten the defender. A follow-up thrust has an excellent chance of success.

2

What to Attack and Where to Defend

Knowing your own strengths and an opponent's weak points is crucial if you want to win an armed fight.

Which body parts are most vulnerable depends on the weapon in hand. As a general rule, pointed weapons are most effective against the torso where they can penetrate deeply and damage internal organs. Sharp implements can be used to cut anywhere on the body, but most cuts are not immediately disabling. Unless an artery or the tendons controlling a limb are severed, a cut will probably not take an opponent immediately out of the fight. It is also possible that he may not immediately realize he has been cut.

The impact of a blunt weapon, or a bullet, will definitely be noticed. Blunt weapons can cause trauma to soft tissues but are highly effective against bone. The head is a primary target for any weapon that causes significant impact, as even if there is no serious damage, 'brain shake' can cause unconsciousness. Bullets obviously cause serious damage wherever they hit, but in many ways they are much like pointed weapons; if a bullet does not strike a vital organ then it may not stop the target.

The human body is extremely resilient in some areas and frighteningly vulnerable in others. Attacking the right place can make the difference between slightly hurting an opponent and totally defeating him.

The Body: Vulnerable Areas

The dark-shaded areas here are extremely vulnerable to hard physical attack, particularly the head and neck. The genitals and limb joints are other points to target, without the potentially lethal effects of the other areas.

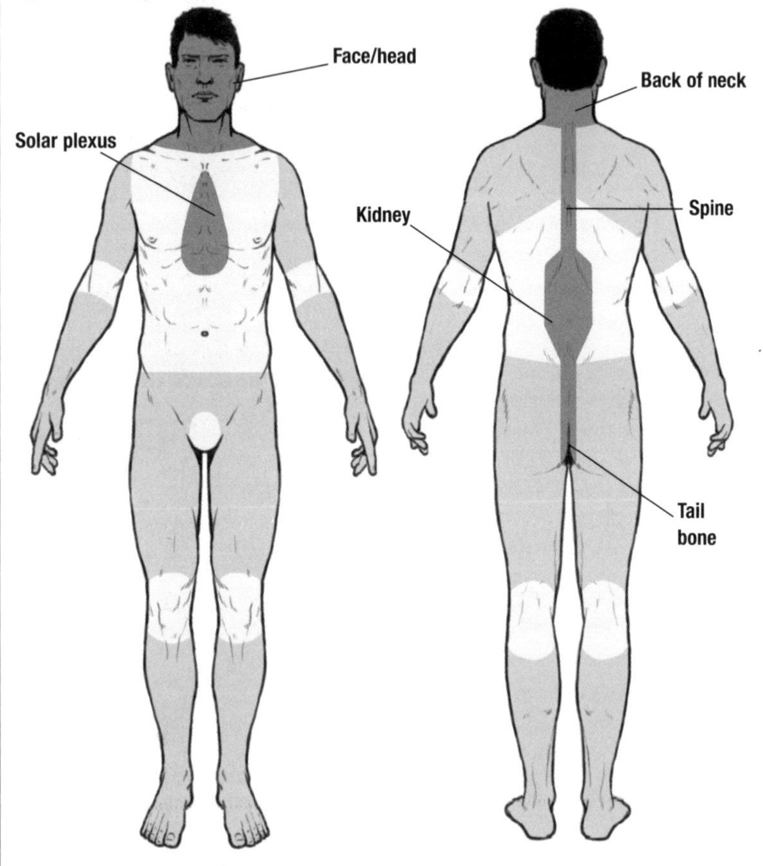

However, any weapon can be used to attack any target, and usually it is better to land a blow that causes relatively little harm than not to land one at all. The target chosen is often a matter of what can be hit – i.e. what body parts are within reach and unprotected by armour, helmets or heavy clothing.

Head and Neck

Any attack to the head is a serious matter and it is therefore the preferred target for many opponents. Even untrained people will tend to attack the head, as it is the seat of consciousness and everyone knows, at an instinctive level, that a successful headshot will put an opponent out of the fight. Strikes to the face also have a significant psychological effect and can cause an opponent who may not actually be hurt very badly to retreat or panic.

The head is generally easier to reach with hand-to-hand weapons than the body or legs, since most blows are swung overhand and the weapon user's arms are high on his body. It is much harder to hit the

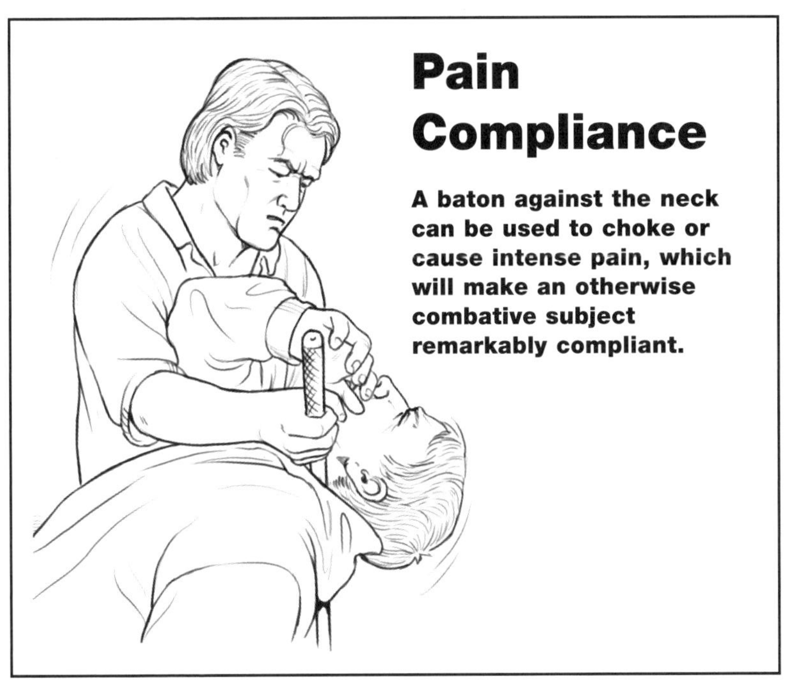

Pain Compliance

A baton against the neck can be used to choke or cause intense pain, which will make an otherwise combative subject remarkably compliant.

head with a stabbing weapon or projectile, as it is relatively small and moves rapidly unless the target is caught unaware.

Blows to the head can cause disorientation and unconsciousness, and heavy impacts can fracture the skull and possibly lead to death sometime after the fight. This makes the head an ideal target with blunt weapons and heavier cutting implements that have a lot of impact, whereas lighter cutting weapons are more effectively employed against the neck. A slash across the face might not stop an opponent, whereas he will collapse and die rapidly if the large blood vessels in the neck are opened.

Rear Knife Defence

Against a rear knife-to-the-throat threat of this sort, best chance is to immobilize the weapon arm and pull it away from the throat before attempting to throw the opponent over your shoulder onto the ground in front of you.

Stabs to the head or face are unusual and are often defeated by the skull, even if head protection is not worn. Most soldiers or police officers involved in a close-range firefight will not shoot for the head if other targets are available. It offers a highly probability of a 'one-shot stop' but is very hard to hit. Snipers or those with time to aim carefully might take a headshot, as might someone who has no better target, but shooting for the head against a rapidly moving opponent is likely to result in a miss.

Thus the head is a primary target for weapons that move in an arc (blunt and heavy sharp implements) and less attractive as a target for projectiles and pointed weapons.

Torso

The torso is slightly harder to hit than the head with hand weapons, requiring an attack to be launched from somewhat close range. It is also easily defended with the arms. Often a fighter will get an arm in the way of a body shot by accident while trying to make an attack of his own. The torso is also fairly well protected by skin (which is thicker than most people imagine), muscle and bone, even if armour or heavy clothing is not being worn.

The torso, or 'centre of body mass', is the primary target for firearms. This is mainly due to it being the easiest place to hit, but the likelihood of striking a vital organ is also an important consideration. Indeed, sometimes security personnel will deliberately shoot for the legs to disable an opponent, as any hit on the torso can be fatal. This applies mainly to situations where the shooter has an opportunity to consider less lethal options; in a firefight or when an opponent is rushing forward with a weapon, centre of body mass is the best target as it offers the greatest chance to hit and stop the target.

Vital Organs

Most vital organs (such as the heart, lungs and liver) are fairly high in the torso, protected by the ribs and thick muscles. These offer relatively little protection against a bullet but can defeat a cutting or short pointed weapon, or a light blunt implement. A shallow stab or cut along the ribs is painful and messy but unlikely to be fatal; it might well not stop the opponent at all. Similarly, the torso can absorb a reasonable amount of blunt force trauma without undue harm.

However, a heavy blunt instrument will break ribs, making breathing difficult, or fracture the collarbone and render the arm on that side useless. This is often a secondary intention with blunt-weapon swings at the head; if the head is missed and the blow lands on the shoulder, it will still do significant damage.

Focus Point

It is wise not to focus your attention on any one part of the opponent, but instead to rest your eyes roughly on the spot marked 'X'. Peripheral vision picks up movement better than direct vision, so you will actually be more aware of what the opponent is doing by not staring at him directly in the face.

Groin Hit

A blow to the groin is not necessarily an instant fight-ender, but it will almost always cause the opponent to react defensively. Often he will bend forward, breaking his posture and making him vulnerable to additional attacks.

Lower in the abdomen are the intestines and, at the rear, the kidneys. The latter are vulnerable and a strike is often disabling and can potentially cause internal bleeding, whereas a frontal strike is less likely to be serious. Not only do the abdominal muscles offer some protection, a low torso strike is also less likely to result in a disabling injury. Bleeding in the low abdomen is less serious than higher in the chest cavity, unless one of the major arteries connecting to the legs is hit.

Hits to the groin are potentially very serious, and tend to have a major psychological effect even if they cause little actual damage. The genitals are surprisingly difficult to hit, not least because everyone knows how painful a blow can be and will inevitably have gained experience of protecting the groin

Combat Gear

Few hand-held weapons will cause much harm through body armour, and even most firearms will not penetrate. Similarly, the soldier is well protected against overhead blows. Someone taking a wild swing at him with a weapon would have little chance of success, though a better-trained opponent might be able to pick a vulnerable target.

from sport injuries, the occasional fight or just painful incidents in daily life. This can be exploited by a smart fighter. An apparent intent to kick or strike the groin can draw an opponent's attention down, leaving his head exposed. The groin also contains large blood vessels that are vulnerable to a stabbing or cutting attack.

The torso is a primary target for pointed and projectile weapons, and less so for blunt implements. Sharp weapons can be effective against the torso, but obtaining a telling hit is often problematic and the result is often a shallow cut that will not immediately stop an opponent.

Legs

The legs are quite difficult to attack with hand weapons as this requires coming in relatively close, which can draw an intercepting strike. A fighter who reaches in deep to strike the legs and is hit in the head while doing so is not getting a good bargain. The legs also contain large muscles that protect them from damage to a great extent. However, these muscles can be a useful target, such as striking an opponent in the legs with a baton to weaken him and cause pain without any real danger of a life-threatening injury.

The knees are, to some extent, the weak point of the leg, but this applies mainly to kicks directed at them from the front or side. With a weapon, it is more common to cut or strike at the muscles unless a lethal attack is intended, in which case a cut to the inside of the thigh can sever the femoral artery and cause the target to bleed out in seconds. Stabs to the legs are likely only by accident.

The legs are not a primary target for any weapon, unless the user is trying to disable the opponent without killing him or they are the only target available.

Arms

The arms are, to a great extent, the easiest target for cutting and blunt weapons, as they are often nearer than any other body part and are 'outside' the torso and head, i.e. a swinging attack may well find an arm before it reaches the torso or head. The arms are not a good target for stabbing or shooting attacks, as they are hard to hit.

Arms have less muscle to protect them and contain smaller bones than the legs, and thus are easier to disable. A blunt weapon strike can break arm bones or disable a hand fairly easily, and even if a cut does not sever tendons it can make an arm useless by parting a muscle. Cuts to the arm can be lethal, especially if the brachial artery in the upper arm is hit. This artery is on the inside of the arm to protect it, but can be targeted if the defender puts up an arm to protect his head, or an attacker overextends on his own strike.

The hands are quite hard to hit but can sometimes be struck by accident, or deliberately 'sniped' with a heavy implement. Broken fingers or damage to the back of the hand makes holding a weapon difficult, and can be used to end an armed confrontation in a non-lethal manner.

Objects held in the hands are similarly difficult to target. Even marksmen would not attempt to shoot the gun out of an opponent's hand under most imaginable circumstances. Occasionally, an

Handgun Disarm

The soldier has moved to the side, where he can exert leverage against the opponent's arm and wrist. He is obeying the 'both hands on the wheel' rule for weapon disarms – control the weapon hand with both of your own. Whatever the opponent's other hand is doing will be less important than making sure he does not shoot or stab you.

opportunity may arise to strike or shoot the opponent's weapon, for example by striking downward with a heavy implement to knock the weapon out of the opponent's hand. However, this is a risky gambit and would normally be undertaken only if the chances were good. As with head shots, in the middle of a desperate fight even a very skilled soldier or police officer would aim at high-percentage targets such as the head and body; there is no place for finesse in the middle of life-and-death combat.

The arms are a primary target for weapons that move in an arc, e.g. sharp and blunt implements. They are not an ideal target, but disabling an opponent's weapon arm will put him out of the fight under most circumstances.

Damage Mitigation vs Damage Elimination

Nobody wants to get hit, and certainly not with a weapon. However, there are occasions where the risk of being hit and injured is considerable, and 'damage elimination', i.e. ensuring that you are not hurt at all, is not always practicable. It may even be counterproductive; it is often necessary to accept some risk of injury in order to have a chance to win.

The exception is the situation where it is possible to withdraw (or flee) from combat. There is no dishonour in retreating from a fight you are likely to lose, especially one that has nothing to do with the mission at hand. For a military Special Forces team, this can mean breaking contact with the enemy rather than trying to defeat them in a standup fight. After all, if the team has been sent to gain information on enemy positions, then defeating a pursuit party does not affect the outcome of that mission. Losing to the pursuers might make the mission a failure as well as costing lives. So it is better to withdraw than fight.

Similarly, police officers will wait for backup in many circumstances rather than rush in. This can be a difficult decision to make, especially if innocents are in danger. However, a lone officer might well simply become another casualty, allowing the incident to continue, whereas a larger group will be able to end it. The same applies to civilians facing an armed threat. The 'mission' for most people is to preserve their own safety and that of anyone they are responsible for, not necessarily to deal actively with the threat. If safety is best preserved by withdrawing, not intervening or just plain running away then this may be a good option.

Eliminating Injury

If the mission can be accomplished by withdrawal, then this eliminates the possibility of injury. If it is necessary to fight, however, then it is also necessary to accept the risks and to focus on taking as little damage as possible (damage mitigation) rather than trying to avoid being hurt at all (damage elimination). Obviously, the ideal goal is to avoid being hurt, but sometimes it is necessary to accept a lesser injury to avoid a greater one.

A soldier under fire might hurt himself diving into cover, but this is very much the lesser of two evils

Angles of Attack

The US Army identifies nine broad angles of attack when using handheld weapons. Number five is a lunging attack, which can be either aimed high or low, at vital organs.

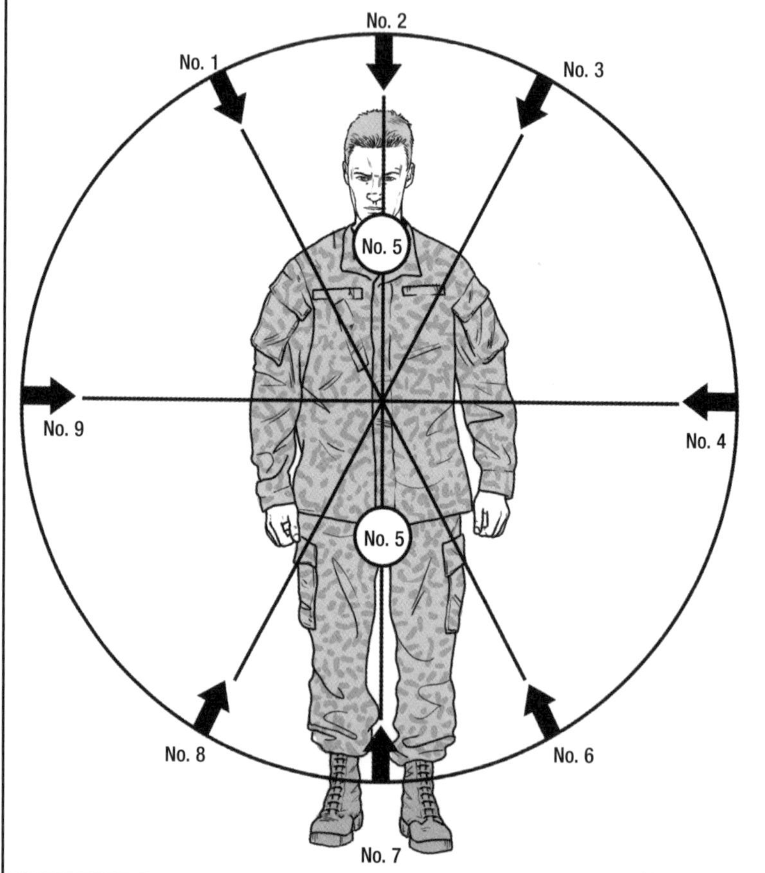

when compared with the prospect of being shot. If he hesitated, fearing scrapes and bruising, he might suffer much worse. So it is with personal combat too. If an attacker is coming forward, swinging a weapon, then it is necessary to accept the possibility of being hit in order to have a chance at defeating him. Constantly retreating in the hope of eliminating damage is ultimately self-defeating.

Unless the assailant gets bored and gives up, he will probably just keep advancing and swinging his weapon; nothing has been gained by retreating. If, on the other hand, the intended target accepts the possibility of being hit and closes in, he now has a chance to fight and win. He may not be hit at all, but sometimes it is necessary to mitigate damage in order to win and avoid worse.

For example, someone who puts an arm in the way of a cut aimed at their neck has traded a painful and possibly serious wound for one that would likely be fatal, i.e. they have mitigated the damage and are still in the fight. An unarmed soldier who defeats a knife-armed opponent but takes two or three small and non-life-threatening cuts in the process has won; if he simply backed away from the knife, he would probably be chased down and attacked anyway.

Damage Mitigation

Damage mitigation on its own is not a winning strategy; curling up in a ball may reduce the amount of injury taken from an enemy beating you with a stick, but there is nothing to stop him from just striking more blows. However, a damage-mitigation rather than damage-elimination strategy is a more realistic response to an armed threat. By accepting the risk of being hurt, and being willing to possibly take a non-fatal wound in order to win, the fighter gives himself the best chance of success.

It is of course possible to defeat an armed assailant without receiving an injury in the process, and, ironically perhaps, it is more likely this will happen if the possibility of a wound is accepted. Most importantly, someone who is not mentally prepared to get hit may panic and stop fighting when they realize they are hurt, even if the injury is fairly trivial.

Overall, a strategy of damage mitigation, i.e. 'try to take as little damage as possible on the way to winning' is a more realistic and usually better option than damage elimination, or 'hope not to get hurt at all'. This does not mean that the soldier actually wants to get hurt, but that he is focussed on winning the fight, not avoiding coming to harm. If he has to take a hit in order to win, then that's a better bargain than not trying to win at all because he was afraid the weapon might hurt him.

Pre-emptive Kick

Kicking the knife out of someone's hand only works in movies, but a kick to the knee can distract the opponent long enough to close in and get the knife hand under control, or may disable the leg and allow a rapid withdrawal out of reach.

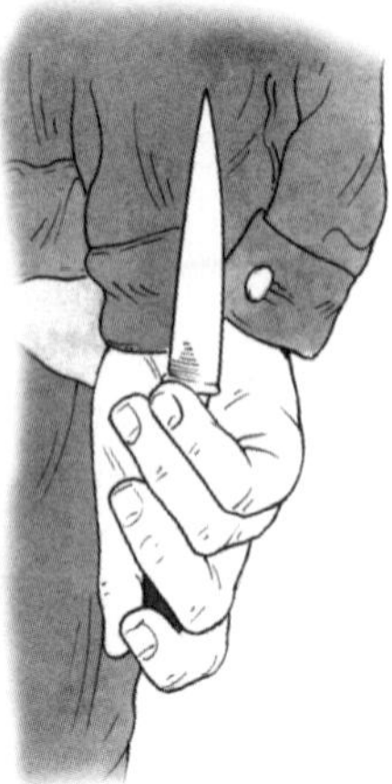

3

Weapon Threat versus Weapon Use

In an armed conflict, contacts with the enemy are characterized by exchanges of fire, which often escalate as additional forces or support elements are brought into play.

However, there are many situations where weapons are used as a threat rather than immediately brought into action. In a security or law-enforcement context, the soldier or police officer's weapon is carried as much for self-defence as for use as a threat. However, the two do overlap. If a police officer attempts to detain a suspect who then attacks him, then the weapon will be brought into play. The fact that the officer is armed might well deter that assault.

This can be a very passive – and, for want of a better word, polite – sort of threat. The officer is openly carrying a weapon but not actively threatening to shoot anyone; arguably the weapon is no threat to anyone but the 'bad guys'. Yet the implicit threat is there – try to fight with this person and they will deploy a lethal weapon. The same goes for military personnel on patrol in a troubled part of the world. Their demeanour and intentions may be friendly as they chat with locals and generally try to keep the peace, but their weapons are a strong hint that interference will not be tolerated.

Weapons carried by personnel engaged in such duties are a threat only to those with ill intent. To law-

Weapons can be used to cause harm, or as 'bargaining chips' in a confrontation.

A Hold Up

In many cases it is better to surrender property than to take on bad odds. If the robbers want money or the car, that's a cheap price for your life. If, however, they were intent on murder or abduction then fighting might well be a better option.

abiding citizens they are often a source of reassurance – the people whose job it is to protect them are present, visible and armed. This passive threat/reassurance is an important part of peacekeeping and security (including law enforcement) operations, and is for the most part implicit. The weapons are there if needed, but there is no active threat.

Lethal Force

Active threats are a different matter. If a police officer has to draw his sidearm or a soldier on security duty deploys his weapon, there is a very real threat to the subject; non-compliance or open attack will be met with lethal force. As noted elsewhere, the presence of a weapon and a credible threat that it will be used can end a situation without violence – someone who is outgunned or whose opponent 'has the drop on him' will usually surrender without shots needing to be fired.

Surrendering to uniformed personnel engaged in security or law enforcement duties is normally a safe option. There are regimes in the world where the police and army are tools of brutal governments, but for the most part someone detained at gunpoint by police or soldiers will be humanely treated – the uniforms our police and soldiers wear are to a great extent a guarantee that they are the good guys.

However, there are occasions where surrendering to an armed opponent does not guarantee good treatment, or even survival. One simple rule is that giving up property to an armed threat, such as a mugger, is often a cheap alternative to risking your life fighting a weapon, but surrendering yourself is never an option. A mugger who demands you

Staying Out of Range

With the exception of firearms, most weapons have a very limited reach. If you can stay out of range then obviously an opponent has to come to you. This can be used tactically, allowing you to determine how he intends to attack – the way he holds the weapon gives strong clues – and to hit him as he closes in. You can also use distance to your advantage by striking the opponent's leg and then backing off. Every step he must take will weaken him physically and mentally, increasing your advantage.

No Guarantees

There is no guarantee that giving up property will keep you from harm. Some criminals will cut or stab their victims even after getting what they want, so throwing down property (rather than handing over) and then quickly fleeing is a sensible option.

hand over your wallet and is satisfied with that is one thing; someone who tries to take you somewhere at weapon point probably intends something more serious than robbery.

Knowing When to Run

Unless there is some pressing reason to fight an armed opponent, escape is the best option. One useful gambit is to throw down whatever they are demanding and take off running when they reach for it. The attacker has a choice between picking up the loot and giving you a headstart, or coming after you immediately. That can make a difference.

As a general rule, someone who shows a weapon to the victim wants something from them, other than to immediately inflict harm. Most armed attacks intended to cause harm do not begin with threats; they are more akin to assassination attempts. Thus someone who means to kill with a knife will normally conceal it and attempt to stab the victim without opposition; someone who wants money (and who is not intending to simply take it off a corpse) will have to show the weapon and make demands.

This does not mean that someone who is waving a weapon around and making demands will not use it, especially if attacked. A high proportion of stabbings and other weapon-inflicted injuries occur after an escalating confrontation. That could be a robbery-gone-bad or perhaps an altercation where one of the people involved deployed a weapon because they felt they were in danger of losing. These people often do not really intend to use the weapon, but once it is in play they will not fight with other means – someone with a knife in their hand will cut or stab, not kick or punch.

Thus anyone who is threatened with a weapon needs to understand that it will be used if the situation 'goes physical'. The words 'you wouldn't dare...' have been the last ones spoken by far too many people. Police personnel are taught that an armed confrontation should be defused and brought to an end without tackling the weapon if possible, but if the suspect insists on trying to use his weapon then superior firepower is the answer. Tackling an armed opponent with hand-to-hand skills is always an extreme risk and should be avoided whenever possible. A threat gives some options – flight, negotiation, giving up property or obtaining a weapon and trying to deter the attack – but a situation in which the weapon is already in play, or where the assailant's demands are unacceptable, must be treated as a lethal threat.

Weapon Retention

In even quite a short-range firefight, there is relatively little chance that a hostile will attempt to wrestle a soldier's weapon from him. However, when engaging in hand-to-hand combat or at extreme close quarters, such as during a house clearance operation, there is always the possibility that an opponent will try to disarm a weapon user.

This is the reason for the near-obsession with wrist grab attacks in certain Japanese martial arts. The Samurai carried swords, and drew them as soon as trouble threatened. The best way to deal with this was to foul the draw – grab the Samurai's wrist and prevent him deploying his weapon. Conversely, the Samurai knew that if this happened they would likely be killed, so they trained extensively to deal with wrist grabs.

In a serious fistfight, it is highly unlikely that anyone would grab for

Weapon Retention

Military and police personnel are trained to retain their weapons when under physical attack. This is an essential survival skill, but it is sadly not always successful. Every now and then a police officer is murdered with his or her own weapon.

a wrist. For one thing they are hard to get to and keep hold of, and a wrist grab does not do much harm whereas a punch in the face will usually get a better result. Thus in civilian self-defence training, wrist grab defences are mainly useful for dealing with low-level 'nuisance' threats or domestic violence situations where they may be used

Reluctance to Engage

Studies of troops' experiences in World War II indicated that a surprisingly large number of men did not fire their weapons in action. These were not cowards; indeed, many took incredible risks to save injured comrades, and most participated actively in combat other than shooting at the enemy. These men were willing to point out targets, load weapons and pass them to the unit's 'shooters' and to advance in the face of enemy fire. They were not, however, willing to harm other people.

Changes were made in military training after the war to increase the number of 'shooters' in a unit – something that is extremely important in small-unit actions – by enabling soldiers to bypass their natural reluctance to hurt people. This does not turn a soldier into a monster; it merely enables him to do what must be done. The choice about when it is necessary to shoot, and when not, remains the same. The only difference is that when it is necessary the soldier can and will use his weapon.

to exert dominance. For the soldier or police officer who goes armed in the course of duty, the wrist grab takes on a greater significance.

Weapon Disarms

Most weapon disarms involve controlling the wrist, and even untrained opponents will grab for the forearm or wrist to try to prevent an officer from using or drawing his weapon. Dealing with such attempts is an essential part of weapon retention training. Police officers are trained to break the grip and push the opponent away, clearing their weapon for action, and to treat any attempt to take their firearm as a potentially lethal threat.

Weapon retention skills apply to all weapons held in one or both hands, not just firearms. The most basic method is to keep the opponent at a distance. Thus personnel moving through a building will not hold their weapon up close to their face and aimed at the ceiling. This is common in television and the movies, probably as a result of close shots of the actor's face intended to increase

Secure the Weapon

Properly trained personnel never leave a weapon close to a downed opponent. At the very least they will kick it away out of reach. If the opponent is determined to hold on to his weapon, stamping on his fingers might be the only way to prevent him from using it.

tension. Police or military personnel using a handgun will keep the weapon quite low and close to the body, enabling them to open doors or fend off a suddenly-appearing hostile with the other hand.

If the opponent cannot be pushed away or intercepted with a blow of the weapon, then the weapon user must free his arm by twisting it sharply and yanking it out of the opponent's grasp. An immobilized weapon is not much use unless the opponent accidentally cuts or impales himself upon it. A firearm can be a hazard to the user, the assailant or anyone else in the vicinity, depending upon where it ends up pointing, but if it is immobilized such that it is not pointing at anyone, then it is no real threat.

If the weapon becomes free and able to move, then it will almost certainly be used immediately. A failed attempt to take a gun away from someone will usually result in being shot as soon as the weapon comes to bear. Sharp implements will often cut as they come free, and sometimes stabbings occur accidentally as a weapon is jerked into motion at the wrong moment.

Handgun Disarm

Twisting a weapon out of the hand is a common component of military disarming techniques. Once the wrist reaches the limit of its movement, the weapon can be levered free. In this case the weapon is gripped by the barrel, ensuring that it does not point in a dangerous direction.

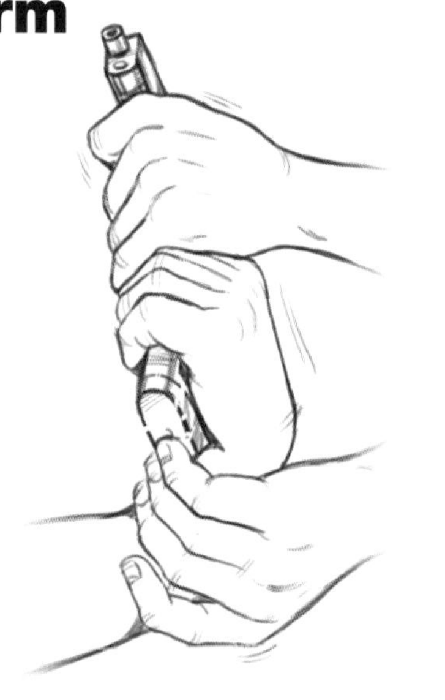

Law Enforcement Tip: Secure the weapon!

If you get a weapon away from someone, secure it. If you cannot keep it yourself, at least put it where it cannot be used, i.e. away from hostiles. Kick it under something or into an inaccessible location, and certainly never leave a weapon close to a hostile who has apparently given up or been disabled. A weapon is a great leveller, and even a mortally wounded opponent can shoot you in the back.

Obviously, the foremost requirement is to keep the weapon from being used, with actually taking it away from the user coming a close second.

For the unarmed fighter trying to immobilize a weapon or obtain control of it, the basic rule is 'both hands on the wheel' – both hands control the weapon or the arm that holds it. If you are being punched in the head with the opponent's other hand then that is bad, but letting go of his knife hand is usually worse. Disarming techniques often look good when demonstrated, but in reality they tend to be a hair-raising, untidy mess. All that matters, however, is success.

'Dirty Tricks'

Most people tend to fixate on the weapon and do nothing but wrestle for it, which may or may not work. Rather than simply struggling for the weapon, trained personnel will try to strike or knee the opponent to distract him from his attempts to gain control, or will use their free hand to push the opponent away. 'Dirty tricks' are often employed for this purpose.

For example, a soldier might push his opponent away with his free hand by the throat or eyes, forcing him to let go of the soldier's weapon hand. Unpleasant as this may seem, it is a better option than letting a hostile take your weapon. There are no rules when someone tries to take away your weapon – he probably means to kill you and other people with it.

Training Safely and Effectively

Training to fight weapon vs weapon, or weapon vs unarmed fighter (either for weapon retention or anti-weapon purposes) can be hazardous. The

Rifle Threat

The soldier uses his lead hand to deflect the weapon, as it is nearest and thus fastest (A). He only has to move it a little to the side to ensure he cannot be shot. He wraps his arm around the weapon behind the muzzle, immobilizing it (B), and attacks the opponent with a groin strike (C).

most obvious rule is not to train with 'live' weapons.

Conducting disarm or weapon retention training with a loaded firearm is just plain stupid, though a blank-firing weapon can be a useful training aid. It will clearly indicate when the weapon would have gone off, allowing the trainees to evaluate whether their technique would have worked, and also allows those training to get used to the sudden noise of a discharge. However, blanks can be dangerous at close range (where training is conducted), so should only be used by properly qualified personnel.

Live (i.e. sharp) knives and other hand weapons should never be used. There is a school of thought that training is not realistic without a live weapon but the risks of injury or even fatality are simply too great. A blunt metal training knife is ideal as it feels

Importance of Training

A common adage among weapons and unarmed combat instructors is 'you fight like you trained, so train how you want to fight'. It is not possible to make training entirely realistic of course, but so far as possible weapons training needs to include some of the stress of combat as well as the technical aspects. The simplest tasks, such as reloading or even remembering to take the safety catch off a weapon become very difficult under stress. Such actions need to become second nature.

Similarly, while it may seem that any reasonably intelligent person could come up with a solution to a given problem on the fly, it is harder than it seems in the middle of a fight. Stress, and the effects of oxygen deprivation on an overworked body that is fighting for survival, can make it impossible to come up with something that would seem obvious at another time. Good training can compensate for this by giving the fighter some simple options that will work under most circumstances.

like a real weapon; floppy rubber martial arts knives will do but are not as realistic.

Real blunt instruments can be used for training, but there is always a chance for an accidental injury. This forces trainees to either be excessively careful, which is not realistic, or ensures that at least occasionally someone will need medical attention. Padded weapons are better as they allow a realistic intent on the part of the user but strikes are merely painful rather than injurious.

A simple rule for training with weapons is that if the equipment

Realism in Training

It is important that training be as realistic as possible without undue risk of serious injury. The attacker in this drill does not limply wave the bat at the defender; he swings it with a fair amount of intent. The defender thus builds confidence in his block and takedown at the same time as practising them.

used is so dangerous that practice must be unrealistically careful then this is counterproductive. On the other hand, weapons used in training must be sufficiently realistic that there is a real feeling of threat. An important part of good weapons training is the necessity to simulate the stress and fear of facing a major threat, and this is not always present with a foam bat or rubber knife. Much depends on the training partner, of course. The perceived threat increases dramatically if the 'aggressor' seems like he is really trying to cause injury.

Every weapon has its own unique characteristics, though certain general principles apply to all weapons within a general class. For example, a stick is a stick to a great extent; it requires the same sort of swing to do any damage. However, its length can significantly influence which moves will be effective with it. The mass and size of a weapon can be very significant; very heavy or large objects are hard to use at close quarters, while very short weapons, such as knives, are outreached by longer weapons.

PART TWO: USING WEAPONS

4

Blunt Weapons

Blunt weapons rely mainly on the delivery of kinetic energy, i.e. the amount of damage they do to the target is determined by their mass and speed at the time of impact.

Some blunt weapons have a degree of flexibility and add a whipping action to their impact; others are inflexible and simply hit hard. Even a fairly small blunt implement, if it is heavy enough, can be used to add impact to a blow or can be used to cause pain by grinding it against the target's body wherever there is bone close to the surface. Blunt weapons are thus highly useful for control and restraint techniques. They will also break bones on a hard enough hit, but this requires enough room for a powerful swing and suitable body mechanics to deliver force.

With some other weapon types, it is possible to deliver an effective strike while the user is off balance, but a good solid stance is essential for effective blunt weapon use. An off-balance user actually weakens his blow as some of the weapon's energy is dissipated in his loose body structure. Ideally, the user's body weight moves with the strike, adding more power to the impact, and the strike is followed-through – i.e. the user tries to hit through the target rather than simply bashing its surface as hard as he can.

Blunt weapons are normally used to land swinging blows, but can also be used to deliver pushing or jabbing strikes – the latter often unexpected by opponents.

Blunt Weapon One-handed Ready Stance

A blunt weapon is normally used from a weak-side-forward stance, which adds power to a blow as well as preventing an opponent from grabbing the weapon. Stances vary, but often the lead hand is used to fend off anyone closing in on the weapon user.

Sticks

Sticks come in various shapes and forms. Many stick fighters consider the ideal length to be from the user's armpit to his fingertips, but it is not always possible to choose a perfect weapon when grabbing an implement from the ground in the middle of a fight. Nevertheless, stick-fighting skills are common to most stick-like implements. This means that training with stick weapons is one of the most versatile skillsets obtainable. It is not always possible to take the weapon with you wherever you go, but you will always have your skills and a suitable implement can usually be found.

Variations on the basic stick concept include side-handled batons, telescopic batons and the like. Most can be used with basic stick technique, and give some additional capabilities. For example, the side-handled baton can be used to hook or trip an opponent, or gripped by the side projection and used to block attacks with the forearm. Ultimately, however, stick weapons are for hitting people with.

Most users will strike with a point about a third of the way down the weapon from the tip, robbing them of some of its reach. A skilled stick fighter may instead 'feed the tip', i.e. using wrist motion to deliver a strike with the very tip of the weapon. This works best with a stick that has a little flexibility, as its whipping action adds to the impact.

Forehand Strike

The most basic of all stick strikes is the forehand blow, usually delivered diagonally downwards towards the side of the head, the shoulder or the opponent's arm. A forehand blow can also be delivered to the legs or

Trainers Tip: In Range When You Want To Be

The only reason for being within striking distance of an opponent is to enable you to strike him. If you are not intending to attack imminently, or at least want him to think you are about to strike, get out of range. Even a total incompetent might hit you by accident if you are within range and doing nothing.

Two-handed Ready Position

The commonest two-handed ready position is a weak-side-forward stance similar to that used with a one-handed weapon. A more square-on 'neutral' stance is sometimes used, not least because it holds the weapon ready in a fairly non-threatening manner.

Forehand Strike

The basic forehand strike is a simple movement, normally made diagonally from above the right shoulder with the weapon 'rolled' forward with the wrist. The weapon starts in an upward position and is turned forward towards the target during the strike. With a light blunt weapon it is the wrist that supplies most of the weapon's velocity.

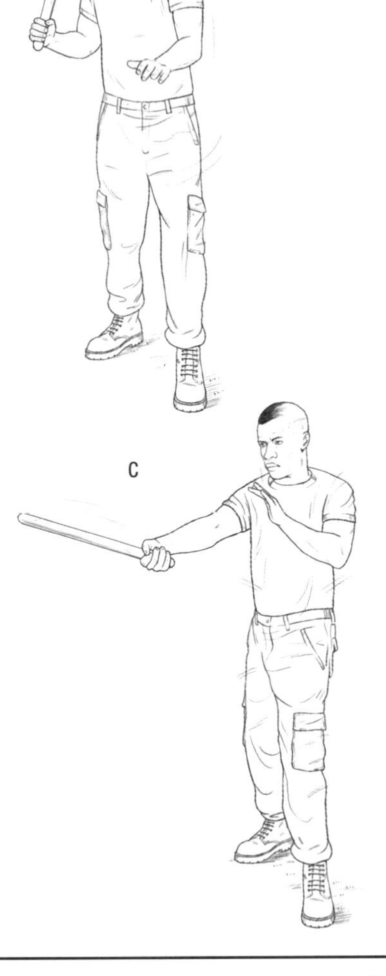

Backhand Strike

A backhand strike comes from over the weak-side shoulder and is made with a straightening action of the arm, with the wrist turning to accelerate the weapon as it nears the target point.

A

against a weapon, hopefully knocking it from the opponent's grasp. Forehand strikes can also be delivered horizontally into the opponent's ribs, or even upwards, perhaps into the underside of the arm. The downward strike is the most common, however, as it makes use of gravity as well as the body's own internal mechanics.

Backhand Strike

A backhand strike is also delivered diagonally downwards against much the same target. It often follows a missed forehand strike as the weapon's momentum carries it into a ready position for a backhand blow. It is not uncommon for an unskilled stick user to simply wade forward swinging forehand-backhand-

forehand. The backhand position is also sometimes used as a threat by some weapon users.

Backhand strikes can be delivered horizontally or upwards, much as with forehand strikes.

Two-Handed Push Strike

A more sophisticated strike begins with the weapon held at waist height, with one hand near to each end of the weapon. From this position it is possible to deliver a forehand strike with the stick in either grip, by letting go with the other hand and taking a swing. Alternatively, the user can shove the weapon up and forward into the opponent's face. This has relatively little impact but it comes as a surprise and is very painful. As the opponent flinches, he is open to a strike delivered by letting go of one end of the weapon and striking forehand at his head.

Bayonet Strike

Another two-handed strike uses the weapon as if it were a bayonet on a rifle, jabbing the end into the opponent's ribs. This is not a fight-ender but it may wind the opponent and cause him to bend forward or drop his guard. During World War II, commandos were taught to follow up this strike with a rising jab under the jaw, still with both hands on the stick, which would often kill the opponent.

Stick Thrust

Often a surprise to those who think that sticks can only be swung, it can be used to make a one-handed thrust. A blow to the chest is painful and may open up the opponent to a

Two-handed Push Strike

A push strike is used to deliver a sharp blow to the face or perhaps the throat. It will rarely end a fight on its own but will cause an opponent to recoil and open him up for additional strikes. This blow is often used from a two-handed neutral stance.

follow-up; a thrust to the face will usually make him flinch and bring his hands or weapon to protect his head, making a horizontal strike to the body a good follow-up option.

Hammer Strike

If a short length of the weapon protrudes from the base of the hand, it can be used to deliver a 'hammerfist' type strike. This is an ideal close-quarters blow for occasions where there is no room to swing the weapon. Hammer strikes are normally delivered downwards or backhand, usually against the head or shoulders.

Axe, Mace and Bat Weapons

Some blunt instruments are either bigger or heavier than the typical stick or have a weight at one end to add to their force of impact. We consider axes to be in this category since they follow a path similar to most swung implements rather than being used like a lighter sharp weapon. Axe-type weapons might include fire axes, obviously, but also improvised weapons like entrenching tools. Similarly, 'mace'-type weapons might include large wrenches and other heavy implements.

Many heavy weapons are swung using both hands, usually forehand diagonally down or directly overhead and straight down. A fighter armed with a heavy weapon of this sort will normally assume a weak-side-forward stance – if he is right handed, he will put his left foot forward and swing from right to left. Backhand blows are more awkward with a two-handed weapon but may follow a forehand strike.

It is generally easier to 'recover' a heavy two-handed weapon after a missed strike than a similar one swung with one hand, so a fighter using, say, an entrenching tool in both hands can be ready to attack or defend again a lot more quickly than might be expected.

Lighter weapons in this category can be used one-handed. A swing with a wrench, hatchet or spanner held in one hand follows a path similar to that of a stick, but requires more effort to start it moving and will tend to follow through more on a miss. Thus if the target can dodge the swing of a heavy implement, the opponent will usually overextend and be vulnerable to a counterattack.

Two-Handed Forehand Strike

A two-handed strike is normally delivered diagonally downward, or possibly in a flat arc towards the body. This requires a significant wind-up that will be obvious to an alert opponent, creating time to dodge. The weapon user may well step forward and put his whole body into the blow, which can be devastating if it lands.

Two-handed Forward Strike

A stick can be used to deliver a jabbing strike to the face, body or groin. It is important to get body weight behind such a strike. Most opponents will be expecting a swinging strike and will be surprised by this movement.

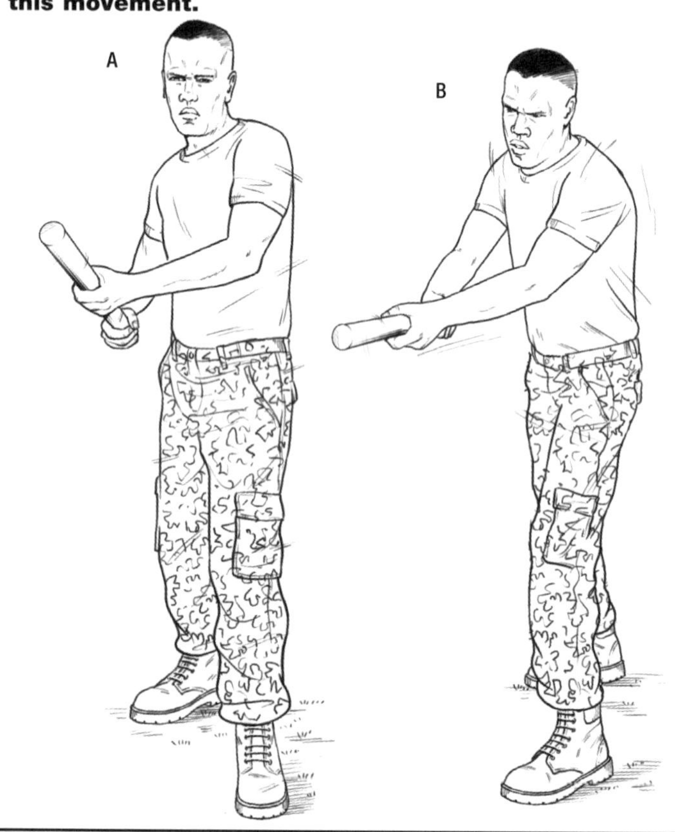

Two-handed Overhead Strike

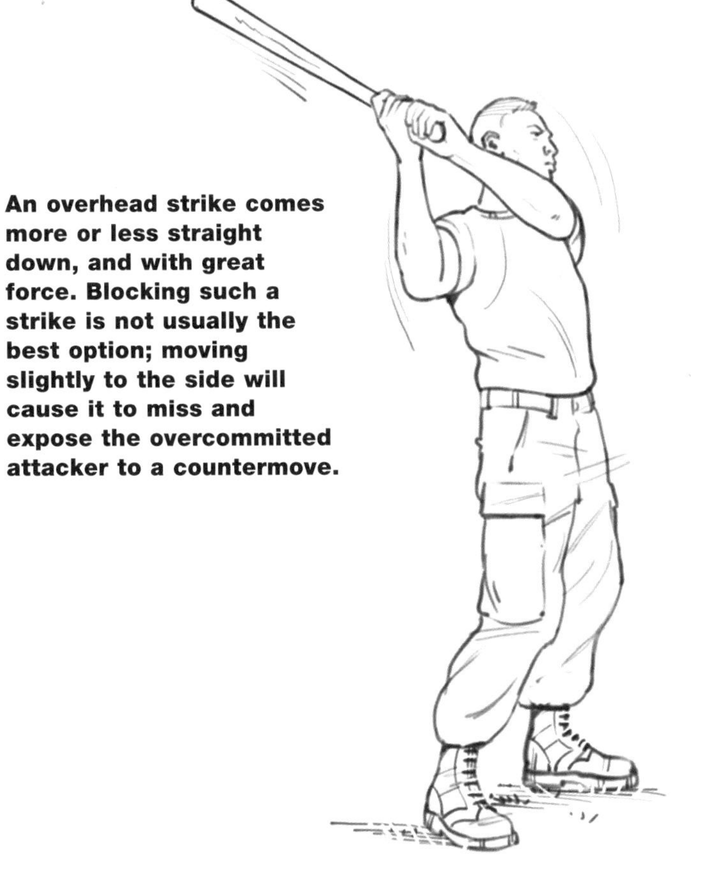

An overhead strike comes more or less straight down, and with great force. Blocking such a strike is not usually the best option; moving slightly to the side will cause it to miss and expose the overcommitted attacker to a countermove.

Two-Handed Overhead Strike
A straight downward strike at the head is an instinctive way to use a two-handed weapon. It is usually pretty obvious what the attacker is about to do, and this is a very committed strike once it is on its way. A weapon user who misses may well hit the ground with his weapon and require some time to recover it for another blow. Overhead strikes are often performed with great aggression while rushing forward to get close enough to strike.

Two-Handed Backhand Strike
Backhand strikes can be a little awkward with two-handed weapons and it is easy to misestimate the distance to the target and miss. A backhand strike will normally follow a forehand strike, with the weapon moving in a figure-eight pattern in front of the user.

Two-handed Forehand Blow

A two-handed swing follows a similar path to a one-handed blow, but on a shorter arc. Putting the weak hand on the weapon reduces its reach but increases the force that can be delivered.

Two-handed Backhand Ready Position

The two-handed backhand ready position is less commonly used than other positions as it is a little awkward, but some opponents will instinctively adopt it as it looks very threatening.

Two-handed Overhead Strike

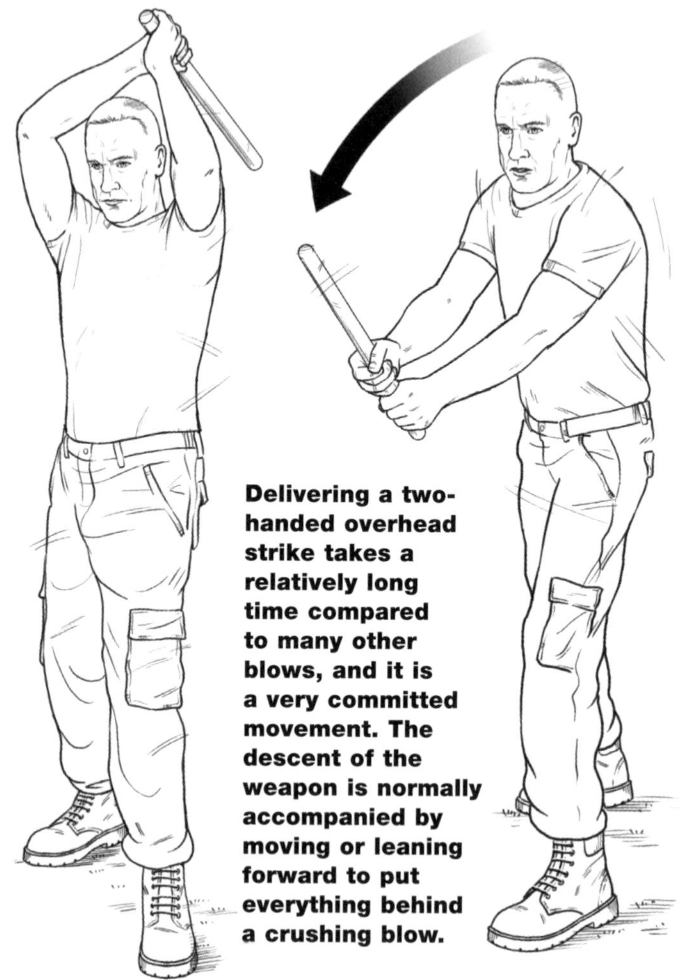

Delivering a two-handed overhead strike takes a relatively long time compared to many other blows, and it is a very committed movement. The descent of the weapon is normally accompanied by moving or leaning forward to put everything behind a crushing blow.

Two-handed Backhand Strike

A two-handed backhand strike is made by straightening the strong-side arm, which supplies most of the force. The weak-side hand supports the strike and assists in getting bodyweight behind the blow, by creating a strong frame at the moment of impact.

Rifle Butt

Even without a bayonet fitted, a rifle or similar weapon makes a useful close-quarters weapon. It is heavy and hard, and can be used to both attack and defend with. The hand position when using a rifle, with one hand near each end of the weapon,

Forehand Butt Stroke

The forehand rifle butt stroke is a forward blow made with moving body weight behind it. The muzzle goes over the weak-side shoulder before the butt is driven sharply out at the target. The weapon is rapidly brought back to a ready position once the strike is completed.

lends itself to moving the rifle in short, vicious arcs that allow the user to switch back to shooting without changing hand position.

A rifle can be 'clubbed', i.e. held by the barrel on both hands and swung like a large club, but this is not ideal. For one thing it makes

it impossible to shoot without reversing the weapon, and at times the muzzle will be pointed at the user. This is never a good thing. Clubbing a rifle places the trigger closer to an opponent than the user, creating many possibilities for disaster.

This method is rarely used by trained personnel equipped with a functional firearm, but it might be encountered from time to time. Someone desperate, incompetent or enraged enough to grab a rifle or shotgun by the business end and start swinging it is an opponent to be wary of; there is no telling what he might do next.

Forehand Butt Stroke

Holding the rifle by the barrel and the handgrip or the base of the stock, the user pivots it forward in a short arc. The butt end hand (usually the user's right) pushes forward while the barrel end is pulled back and may pass over the user's shoulder. The head is usually targeted, but a body blow can also be highly effective.

Jabbing Butt Stroke

A jabbing stroke uses the butt of the rifle to thrust with, usually downward. This action can be directed at the face or body, and can be done to drive an opponent back or simply to inflict harm. A jabbing stroke often follows a forehand strike, with the weapon barrel over the user's weak-side shoulder (usually the left) and then thrust down and forward. The weapon then returns to a shooting position.

Defending with a Blunt Weapon

A blunt weapon can be used to defend in two main ways, either by blocking the attack or by striking the attacker's weapon arm. This is an example of interception, discussed earlier, and is often accompanied by some degree of evasion. Striking his arm as he attacks may put him out of the fight or at least render him vulnerable to a follow-up.

A strike against the opponent's weapon arm is an opportunistic offensive-defence, requiring that the defender be alert and have his weapon ready. This requires a certain amount of skill, as the weapon arm will be moving quite fast, but at least it will be travelling along a predictable path. A counterattack of this sort is carried out with any of the weapon's usual strikes, such as a forehand or backhand blow, and has the advantage that an opponent in the process of making an attack will probably not be ready to defend.

More commonly, blunt instruments are used to block an attack, after which a strike is launched. Blocking is simply a matter of putting the weapon in the path of the strike, but there are a few basic principles that must be observed. The hand is weak in some directions and strong in others; it is thus necessary to ensure that a block is carried out in a 'strong' direction to avoid losing the weapon.

For example, if a stick-armed fighter holds his weapon out with his palm down and an opponent strikes it sharply downwards, it may slip out of his grasp. With the hand in almost any other orientation, it would be hard to dislodge it from his grip.

When blocking, the hand is turned so that the force of the blow is travelling into the web of the hand between thumb and fingers. This allows the alignment of the forearm to soak up much of the impact and the fingers to prevent the weapon being twisted out of the user's grip.

Defensive Ready Stance

One way to defend with a stick or similar implement, especially against

Defensive Ready Stance

A defensive ready stance is often used by police and security personnel. The lead hand is not just defensive; it acts as a psychological barrier and adds weight to a command to surrender or remain at a distance. An incoming opponent can be 'checked' with the lead hand at a perfect distance to be hit with the baton.

Strong Direction/ Weak Direction

The hand is stronger in some orientations than others. In figure A, the defender's hand is at its strongest and well able to resist the blow as the force goes into the palm. In figure B, the force is mainly directed against the thumb, and can lever the weapon out of the user's hand. Many defences use this position with great effectiveness, but there is always a greater chance of being disarmed when the hand is in its weak orientation.

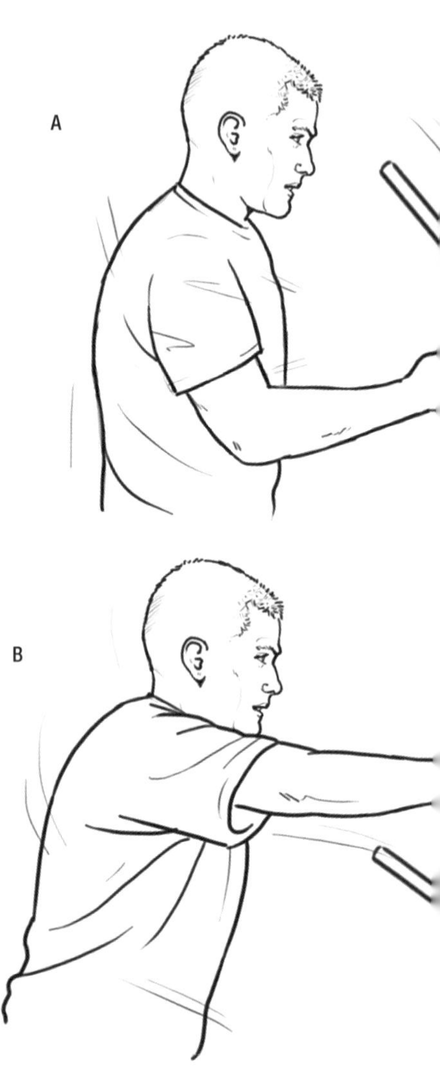

Stick Blocks

Blocking an attack with a stick involves as little movement of the hand as possible. The length of the stick is used to place it where it is needed, keeping the hand in a fairly small 'box' in front of the defender's torso. The less the hand has to move, the quicker the block and the less likely the defender is to be drawn out of his defensive position and exposed to a strike he cannot get to in time.

Cross-body stick down block

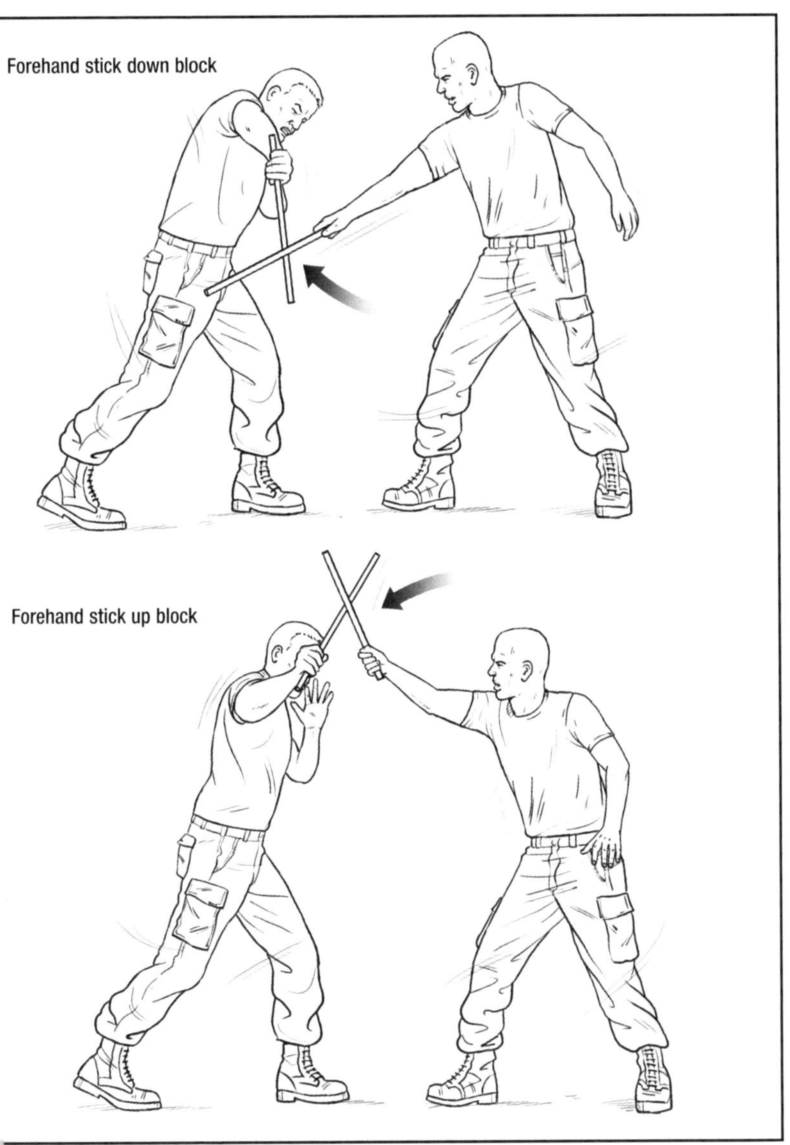
Forehand stick down block

Forehand stick up block

unarmed fighters, is to keep the opponent at a distance and use the stick as a threat. A standard posture used by many police forces is the defensive ready stance. The stick is 'chambered' ready for a forehand strike, but lies over the user's shoulder as a very graphic indication of what will happen if an attack is launched. In this position it cannot be grabbed or knocked out of the user's hand.

The stick user's weak hand is extended as both a psychological and physical barrier. An opponent who moves forward to attack can be fended off, or brought to a halt ('checked') with the lead hand and then struck with the stick or baton. An armed opponent will probably just be struck, with the lead hand moved out of harm's way as he advances. The strike can be aimed at the attacker's weapon or weapon-holding arm, or delivered to the head and shoulder as appropriate.

Stick-Up Blocks

From a basic forehand ready position, the most accessible blocks are made with the stick pointing upward. Against an attack coming in from the stick user's left (such as a forehand blow from a right-handed opponent), the block is made by simply pushing the fist (with the stick pointing up out of it) across the body until it meets the incoming strike. Once the strike has been halted, the defender rolls his hand over into a backhand position and then delivers a blow to the opponent's head.

Against a blow coming in from the right (such as a backhand strike by a right-handed opponent) the defender can simply stay in his forehand defensive position, pushing the fist (with the stick pointing up out of it) a little to his right to absorb the impact. To follow up, the defender then raises his hand and delivers a diagonal downward forehand strike.

Stick-Down Blocks

Against a low attack to the legs, the hand holding the stick is turned over so that the stick is pointing down. Against a forehand strike (coming in from the left against a right-handed stick user), it is pushed across the body to meet the incoming blow, and once the strike has been blocked a backhand blow is delivered.

Against a backhand blow (coming in from the right against a right-handed stick user), the stick is rolled over in a semicircle to point down and swept out to meet the strike. Afterwards, the hand is raised and the stick turned 'up' again, and a forehand strike is delivered.

Leg Slip

As an alternative defence against strikes to the legs, it is possible to 'slip' the target leg – move it back out of reach while keeping the body

Blunt Weapons Tip

Most people will make big, heavy swings with a blunt weapon, and tend to hit at a point about one-third of the way down the weapon. This shortens the reach of the weapon considerably. With lighter sticks, it is better to 'feed the tip' and use wrist motion to strike with the tip of the weapon. This increases both reach and impact.

forward and launching a counter strike to the attacker's head or arm.

Overhead Blocks

Stick-up blocks work well against a diagonal downward attack, though it may be necessary to raise the hand and angle the block to meet the strike. Against an attack coming in at a more vertical angle, especially attacks that are delivered straight down, an overhead block is more useful.

A direct overhead block can be made with one or both hands on the weapon. Both hands may be used to absorb a very heavy strike (though often it is better to evade such a blow) or when using a weapon normally held in both hands, such as a rifle. This block is made by holding the defensive implement horizontally and pushing it upwards into the path of the attack. It can be followed up with a jabbing butt stroke or, depending on the weapon, by taking one hand off it and delivering a forehand strike.

With a stick or similar weapon normally held in one hand, a better option is an angled stick-down block, which allows the opponent's strike to slide off the end of the weapon and continue downwards, often causing him to overextend. The defender can use a hammer strike to follow up, or a forehand blow. Alternatively, the defender can bring his unarmed hand into play to immobilize the opponent's weapon hand.

To do this, the defender makes an angled stick-down block and reaches towards the opponent with his unarmed hand, ensuring that his arm is 'inside' the protection of his block. The free arm then snakes over and around the opponent's weapon arm and immobilizes it, while the weapon hand delivers hammer strikes with the base of the defender's weapon.

Leg Slip and Counter Strike

Attacking the legs requires reaching in deep, exposing the head to a counter strike.

One effective counter is to move slightly back out of reach, then, as the opponent's weapon goes past (but before he can recover to a defensive stance), lunge in and strike his exposed head. An alternative tactic is to strike the extended arm.

Two-handed Overhead Defence with Counter-strike

If a heavy overhead blow has to be blocked, then a solid stance and two-handed defensive grip are advisable. The blocking implement is pushed up to meet the descending weapon.

As the opponent recoils from the heavy blow, the defender releases one end of his own weapon and delivers a sharp forehand strike to the head.

A
B

Overhead Stick Down Block with Follow-up Strike

A heavy forehand blow can be blocked by resting the blocking weapon against the defender's shoulder (in [A] and [B], shown from both sides). The weak-side hand can be used to grab the opponent's weapon arm and immobilize it while a counter strike is launched [C].

5

Knives and blades are some of the most commonly held weapons, primarily because they are easy to obtain and conceal.

Sharp and Pointed Weapons

Some weapons, such as knives, are both sharp and pointed, i.e. they can be used to cut or stab. How the weapon is held at any given moment will indicate to the experienced fighter what the user is about to do – the mechanics of a slash are quite different to those of a cut.

Some knives are only useful for cutting, such as Stanley knives or box cutters – a thrust with such a blade is quite unlikely. Many larger cutting implements, such as machetes, are not well suited to thrusting attacks and will normally be used to cut with. At risk of splitting hairs, there are two types of cutting attack:

Hack A 'hack' is a hard swing with a heavy bladed implement, using the mass of the weapon to drive the edge into the target. A hacking cut can be pushed or drawn (pulled back towards the weapon user) after impact for an additional cutting action, but it is the impact of the edge, biting deep into the target, that does the most damage.

The mechanics of cutting and thrusting are quite different, and the wounds inflicted also differ. A cut is far less likely to be immediately fatal than a stab wound, but is often easier to inflict.

Kenjutsu Guard Pose

The Japanese sword arts rely largely on well-timed attacks and evasion to protect the swordsman, and use a primarily offensive ready stance. Western swordsmanship makes greater and more effective use of parries with the blade, and is more defensive in nature. Indeed, the term 'fencing' comes from the term 'defence'.

Slash A 'slash' is a sliding, slicing action designed to make best use of the cutting action of the weapon's edge. Slashing attacks must be pushed or drawn after making contact, i.e. the blade must slide in contact with flesh if any real damage is to be done.

Some heavier, 'hacking' blades can be very sharp and will still cut if simply laid on the victim's flesh and pulled or pushed, but most do not cut all that well when used in this manner. A heavy blade then cannot move much is a greatly reduced threat. Lighter blades do not cut well at all unless they are kept very sharp, but it is wise to assume that any combat weapon is kept in a state of readiness. A nearly immobile combat knife can still cut deep into flesh and need move only a little to cause a serious wound.

Fighting Stance

Other implements may only be useful for stabbing, such as screwdrivers, broken bottles and the like. It might be possible to deliver a very nasty gouge with the edges of a broken bottle, but it is far more likely that the user will push it at the opponent in a stabbing motion.

With most pointed or edged weapons, users may swap from a strong-side-forward to a weak-side-forward stance according to circumstances. Strong-side-forward presents the weapon well forward (assuming it is held in the strong hand, which it almost always is) and close to the target, while keeping the user's head and body back, away from a counterattack.

A weak-side-forward stance has less reach with the weapon but allows the 'off hand' to play a greater part in the fight. This allows it to be used to fend off attacks, to grab the opponent or to protect the weapon itself from a disarm attempt. When using a heavy weapon, the weak side (usually the left) is normally forward to allow a powerful swing. This position is no different to that used with heavy blunt implements.

A fighter may well 'step through' with an attack, moving from a weak-side-forward position to an extended strong-side-forward position, or retire to a defensive weak-side-forward position after a failed attack. An extended stance gives a lot of reach but risks becoming overextended, making it easy to counterattack.

Knives and Similar Implements

Most improvised pointed or sharp weapons are somewhat awkward to use, but follow the same principles as a true weapon. For this reason, we will use the knife as a general example of all pointed or sharp weapons. It is the most versatile of combat tools; there are many things that can be done with a knife that are extremely difficult when using any other weapon, but it is always possible to cut or stab with any edged or pointed implement.

There are two ways to grip a knife. With a conventional grip, the blade protrudes out of the hand in the same direction as the thumb, and is well suited to pushing and slashing actions. Alternatively, a knife can be held in a 'reverse' or 'icepick' grip with the blade protruding from the base of the hand.

Knife Ready Stance

A strong-side forward stance presents the weapon towards the opponent and keeps the body well away from his weapon. A weak side forward stance allows better use of the 'off hand' to deflect attacks or grab the opponent, but requires the confidence to get close before making an attack.

Strong side forward knife

Weak side forward knife

Knife Fighter Stance

Many knife-fighting stances conceal the weapon as much as possible, using the body and the unarmed hand. The unarmed or 'off hand' is actively used for defence and sometimes to grab or strike the opponent.

Strong side forward knife

Weak side forward knife

An icepick grip is sometimes used defensively by knife fighters. It gives some useful options to a trained fighter, but offensively it is more limited than a conventional grip. An icepick grip allows only a downward stabbing action that has far less reach than a conventional thrust, and an inward slashing action that also lacks reach. Many untrained users will take an icepick grip because they have seen it in the movies; in such hands it is far less of a threat than a conventionally held knife.

Conventional Grip: Stabbing Attacks

Stabbing attacks are normally aimed

Head Grab and Upward Stab

An upward stab under the ribs is one of the primary killing blows with a knife. The opponent will try to recoil away, which may prevent deep penetration. Grabbing his head and pulling him onto the weapon ensures the success of the strike.

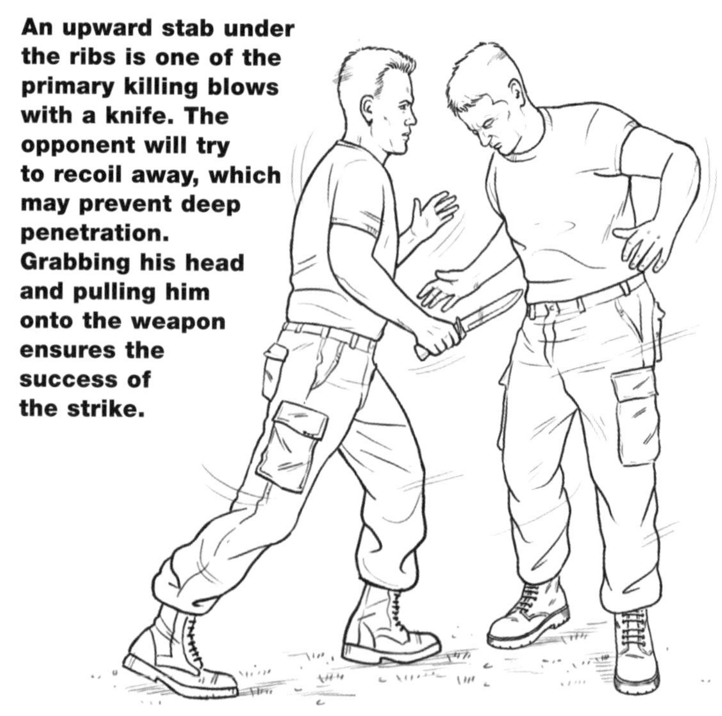

at the front of the torso. Few stabbing attacks are aimed at the head or limbs. Stabs are generally delivered from close range, and as a rule the closer the attacker is to the target, the more difficult it will be to defend.

The most basic knife attack is the upward stab, delivered from a weak-side-forward position with the knife held quite low and thrust slightly upward towards the opponent's torso. Most such attacks are aimed to go in just under the ribs; a knife held vertically will not slip easily between the ribs and may jam or be deflected. If the point of impact is just below the ribs and the blade is

Lunging Stab

The soldier steps through from a weak-side-forward stance into a lunging position, greatly increasing his reach. The danger of such a long, committed attack is obvious; an alert opponent could deflect the strike and counter. However, the attack may come as a surprise if the defender thinks he is out of reach.

angled upward it may find the heart, lungs and associated large blood vessels, causing a rapidly fatal injury.

Many stabbing attacks are relatively poorly aimed and enter the abdomen rather than the chest cavity. This is far less likely to result in an immediate fatality, but knife users will often compensate for this by repeatedly stabbing the victim. A stabbing attack of this sort is generally facilitated by grabbing the opponent and dragging him onto the knife. Once the first stab has gone in, the knife is withdrawn and repeatedly stabbed home with a pumping action, which is extremely hard to defend against even if the victim is not incapacitated.

A variant on this technique is to grab the opponent around the head or neck from behind and stab into the

kidney area, or to deliver a single stab to the kidneys while walking past and to move on quickly as the target collapses. These are not fighting techniques of course; they are assassinations.

An alternative, and less common, stabbing attack is a long thrust with a step through from a weak-side-forward position to an extended strong-side forward stance. Such a strike is normally aimed at the upper torso and covers a lot of distance, but only at the risk of being deflected and countered.

Conventional Grip: Slashing Attacks

Slashes are generally aimed at the head, neck and limbs. The latter often happens more or less by accident, with limbs attacked either

Back Stab

A stab to the kidneys will rapidly disable an opponent, who is likely to then bleed to death. Grabbing his head ensures that the knife penetrates deeply. This is in no way a 'fighting' technique – it is an assassination.

Slashing Attack

Slashing attacks cause significant bleeding. If an artery (for example in the neck or the inner thigh) is hit, then death can occur quickly. A slash to the brow is rarely life-threatening but will blind an opponent with blood and probably intimidate him enough that he seeks escape rather than further combat.

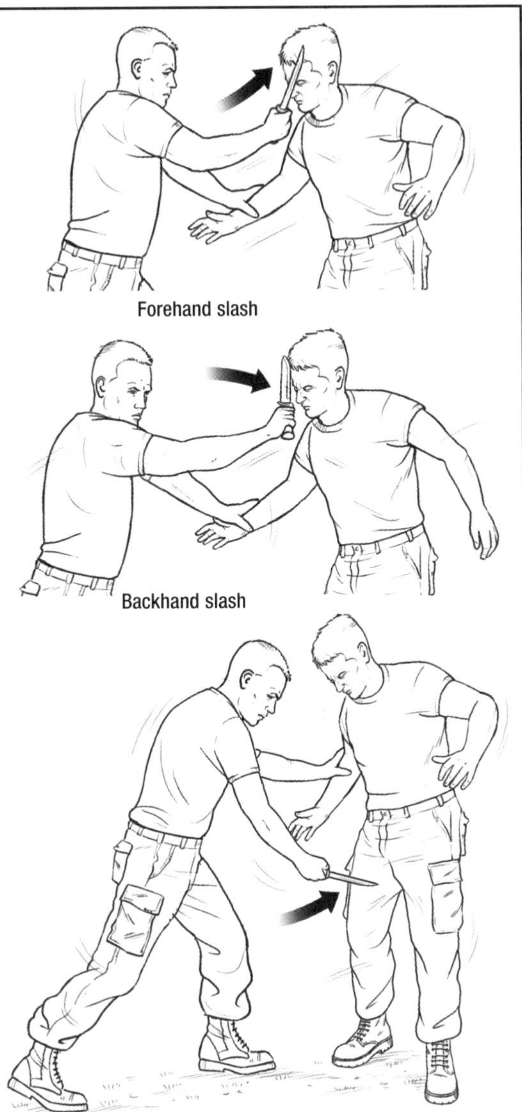

Forehand slash

Backhand slash

Leg slash

Icepick Stab

The icepick stab can be performed with any small pointed implement and is a strong movement making use of the arm's natural alignment. However, it lacks the reach of a more conventional stabbing motion and is best used at extreme close quarters.

as 'targets of opportunity' or because they get in the way of slashes aimed at more vital regions.

The most common slashing attack is a diagonal downward forehand cut to the side of the head, neck or shoulder. The same action can be used to cut at the opponent's arm or, from a low position, at the outside of the body or the leg. The latter is not very effective if it hits the outside of the leg, but a slash across the inside of the upper thigh can rupture the femoral artery and kill in seconds. This technique was used by World War II commandos, taking advantage of the fact that most opponents expected cuts to come in high on the body and were thus unable to defend against it effectively.

A backhand slash is also highly effective, and often follows a forehand cut. The same targets are available, but as a rule a backhand slash made against an opponent who is in a conventional weak-side forward stance will tend to hit the outside of the defender's arm or leg if directed at a limb. A forehand strike is far more likely to hit the inside and open an artery.

Slashing attacks can of course be directed horizontally or diagonally upwards. Since a light knife can change direction very quickly, cuts can be delivered from unexpected angles. It is also possible to assassinate a target, such as an enemy sentry, by grabbing from behind and cutting the throat. There is no possible justification for this in civilian life, but in a war zone it is a valid military tactic.

Icepick Grip

It is relatively difficult to deliver a stabbing attack from an icepick grip. Untrained users may try to drop a massive stab downwards towards the shoulder region, which can be deadly if it lands and is certainly intimidating, but is relatively easy to deal with. Nevertheless, many martial artists train extensively against this sort of attack as if it were the only thing that can be done with a knife.

A far more effective version of this movement is to get close and grab with the weak hand, delivering short strikes with a hammering action. World War II commandos were taught to stab down behind the collarbone, puncturing a major artery and ensuring extremely rapid death. This can be done from in front or behind the target.

Icepick stabs can also be delivered at close range to the chest area, usually with a backhand action. These are short in-and-out blows that may not immediately drop the target unless they hit something vital, but which will cause serious internal bleeding and fairly rapid disablement.

Icepick slashes are also short-ranged attacks, with the weapon often moving in a figure-eight pattern back and forth in front of the opponent. Such cuts tend to be shallow but do not overcommit the weapon user, bringing his knife back into play quickly.

Cuts can also be delivered very deliberately by gripping the opponent with the 'off hand' and hooking his wrist with the knife. Drawing the knife across the wrist will cut tendons and make the opponent's hand useless, causing much pain and taking him out of the fight.

Bayonet Slash

The bayonet slash uses the sharp edge of the bayonet, which is drawn across the target to cause a deep cut.

Mounted Bayonet

A bayonet that is not mounted (attached to the business end of a rifle) is a knife, and the rifle can be used as already described as a pretty good club. Putting the two together creates a versatile close-quarters weapon system that can be used to stab or deliver butt strokes whenever the user is at close quarters, without compromising his ability to shoot.

The long rifle gives leverage to the cut, but it is the drawing action that is important – the bayonet is dragged across the target's flesh, not swung to deliver impact like an axe.

The standard bayonet attack is a two-handed thrust to the body from a weak-side-forward position. It is delivered with extreme force and aggression from a solid stance. It is also possible to cut with the bayonet, but this is awkward and can cause it to come off its mountings. Soldiers have been known to tape their bayonets in place to avoid losing them.

Sword or Machete

There are some parts of the world where it is common – indeed necessary – to carry a large cutting implement such as a machete while going about your daily business. This is normally the case in regions where there is a lot of thick undergrowth or jungle. Machetes are essential to mobility and, most of the time, they are simply tools. However, a heavy cutting weapon like this can deliver serious wounds with ease.

Swords are uncommon today, although the possibility exists that someone will arm himself with one. The sort of swords likely to be encountered in combat fit into two general categories: one-handed and two-handed. Most swords can be used to thrust with, but for the most part they will be used to cut.

One-Handed Swords and Machetes

Long, relatively heavy blades give the user a lot of reach and can deliver powerful cuts. Some sword users will adopt a strong-side-forward stance; some will stand weak-side-forward. A deep fencing-style lunge is unlikely – sword or machete users are more likely to take a step forward with their attack, at most.

Cuts with a heavy blade will likely follow a similar path to blunt-weapon attacks, with diagonally downward forehand strokes being common, along with backhand cuts following a similar line. Stopping such a strike is difficult, as the long blade can cut at any point on its length and it requires a considerable degree of movement to get out of its reach. A block of the same sort as used against blunt weapons is the most effective option for those not trained in swordsmanship.

Those trained in fighting with weapons of this sort often make extensive use of the unarmed hand to deflect attacks or to grab their opponent. This becomes less common, however, as blades get longer – a machete user, for example, is more likely to attempt a grab than someone armed with a broadsword.

Two-Handed Swords

The most likely two-handed sword threat is from someone who has bought a Japanese Katana and decided to run amok with it. The Katana can actually be used in one or both hands, but the sort of person

Two-handed Sword Block

If blocking with a sword or machete-like weapon, the edge is used to meet the edge of the opponent's weapon (as seen here on the left). Trying to parry with the flat or back of the blade can result in a broken or dropped weapon. The cut must be met as close to the hilt of the defender's weapon as possible, as this is the strongest part of the blade.

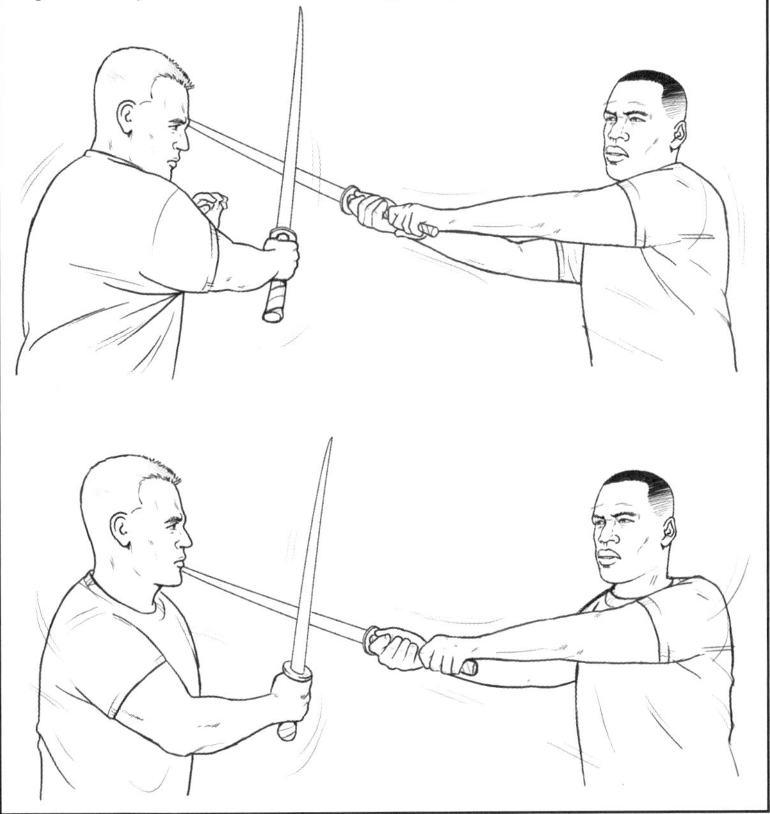

Evade and Counter

Instead of blocking a cut, it may be possible to evade it and launch a counterattack. The opponent's weapon arm is a good target, as it is exposed by his attack. A more sophisticated (and risky) option is to 'stop-cut' the opponent's arm, using an attack against the arm as both defence and counterattack.

likely to bring one to a fight will normally just make big swings with it.

Two-handed swords are normally used from a weak-side-forward posture and attack using similar techniques as a baseball bat – at least, in the hands of an angry or untrained user. The subtleties of Japanese and European swordplay are almost infinite, and beyond this book's scope, so we must consider only the most basic of moves.

A two-handed sword user will normally make a forehand downward cut or a directly downward one, possibly alternating with backhand cuts. These are blocked much like blows with a heavy blunt weapon, with two slight differences. Firstly, swords tend to be a bit lighter than many blunt weapons, so there is less impact to worry about. All the same, a solid stance and good body structure are necessary to absorb the blow.

Secondly, the weapon's edge is still a threat even when it is blocked. An opponent might (deliberately or otherwise) drag or push his weapon around a block in the hope of cutting the defender. Such wounds are less serious than if the weapon were slammed home, but they are still potentially dangerous.

Defending With a Sharp or Pointed Weapon

Small sharp or pointed weapons cannot be directly used to defend against an attack, i.e. putting a knife in the way of a blow will probably not work. For one thing, the small size of the weapon means that a successful block is unlikely – it takes great precision to get a knife blade in the way of an incoming strike. Such a light weapon may not adequately absorb the attack. If it is pushed aside, the blow may come through scarcely weakened.

Thus defence with light, sharp or pointed weapons normally involves deflecting the attack with the unarmed hand, or seizing the opponent's arm, and then countering with the weapon. Alternatively, the defender can evade the attack and then move in for a strike of his own.

Larger weapons can be used to block much like blunt instruments. As already noted, there are many subtleties to swordplay, which are beyond this book, but at the most basic level a one-handed sword or machete can be used to block in the same manner as a stick. Indeed, some martial arts use the stick and machete interchangeably.

Larger weapons, such as a Katana, can be used to make two-handed versions of the same blocks. However, the sort of swords owned by people likely to run amok with them are not of high quality and may break surprisingly easily. Most styles of swordsmanship (European and Oriental) use evasion to weaken an attack at the same time as the blade is put in the way.

The basic principle with most bladed weapons is to turn the 'true edge', the main sharp part of the blade, to meet the attack. This places both the weapon hand and the blade itself in the strongest orientation to resist the attack. A blow that hits the side of the blade can knock it from the user's grasp, or bend or even shatter it.

An alternative to blocking with a bladed weapon is to make a 'stop

Off-hand Deflection, Cut and Thrust

Having deflected a thrust with the 'off hand', the soldier has various options. Keeping hold of the opponent's sword arm to stop him defending, he can cut the neck to kill (A) or the sword arm to disable the opponent. A thrust from this position requires some retraction of the weapon arm to get the point 'on line' (B), but an overarm thrust will penetrate deeply and almost certainly kill the opponent (C).

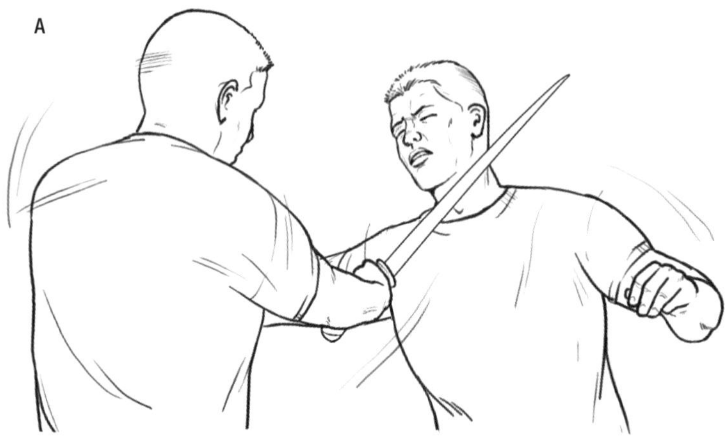

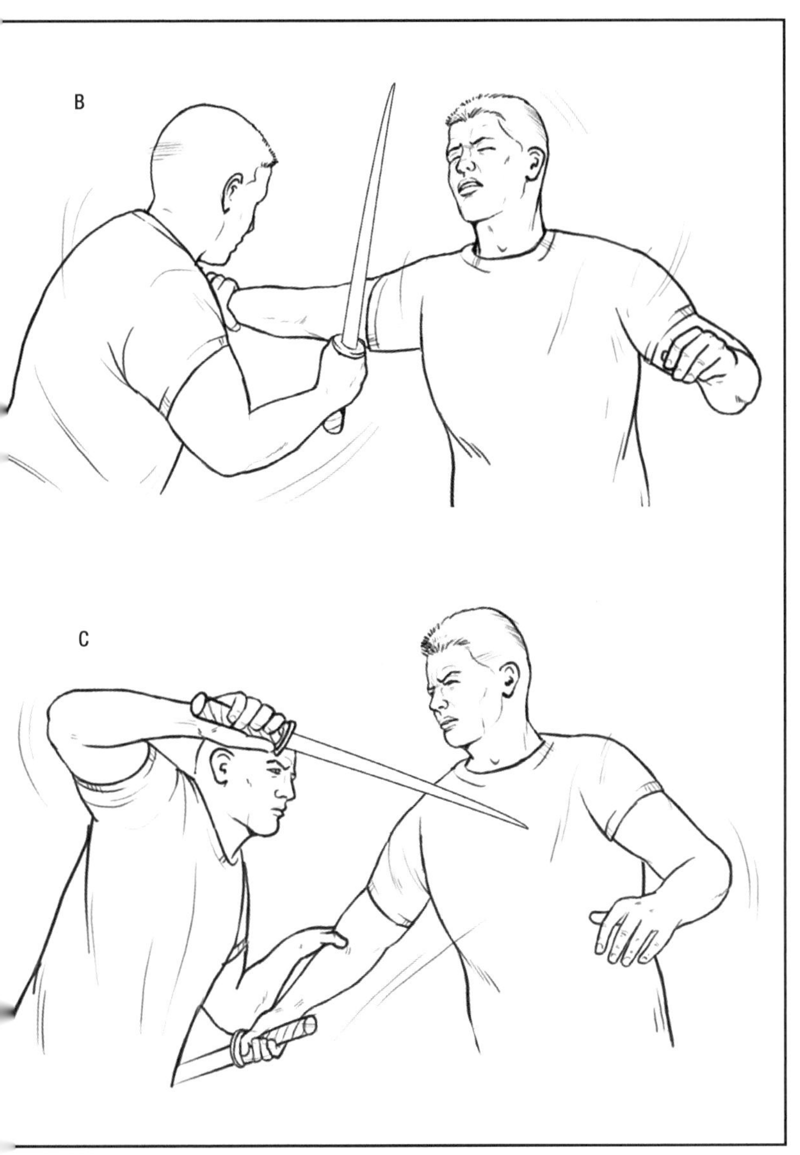
B
C

Stop Thrust

A stop thrust targets the face, throat or chest. The blade is punched out hard from a strong position and the opponent's momentum drives her onto it (A). If the thrust is weak or poorly aimed, the opponent may still be able to reach striking range and land a blow.

A

cut' or 'stop thrust' with it. As the name implies, this is an attack intended to stop that of the opponent. A stop cut is normally aimed at the weapon arm and is accompanied by evasion. Essentially, the opponent's attack is blocked at the arm rather than the weapon, making this an extreme case of offensive defence.

A stop-thrust works when the defender's weapon outreaches that

Against an opponent who foolishly rushes forward, chambering a wild strike, the 'stop thrust' is a viable option (B). As the name suggests, the thrust halts the opponent's forward motion before she can reach striking range. A solid stance and grip on the weapon are essential.

of the opponent, and can be risky. Even a mortally wounded attacker, impaled on the point of a sword or bayonet, could still deliver an attack. When it works, however, a stop-thrust is highly effective. The defender either adopts a solid stance with the point of his weapon aimed at the opponent, or actively thrusts at his head or chest. Either way, the attacker runs onto the point of the weapon as he makes his attack.

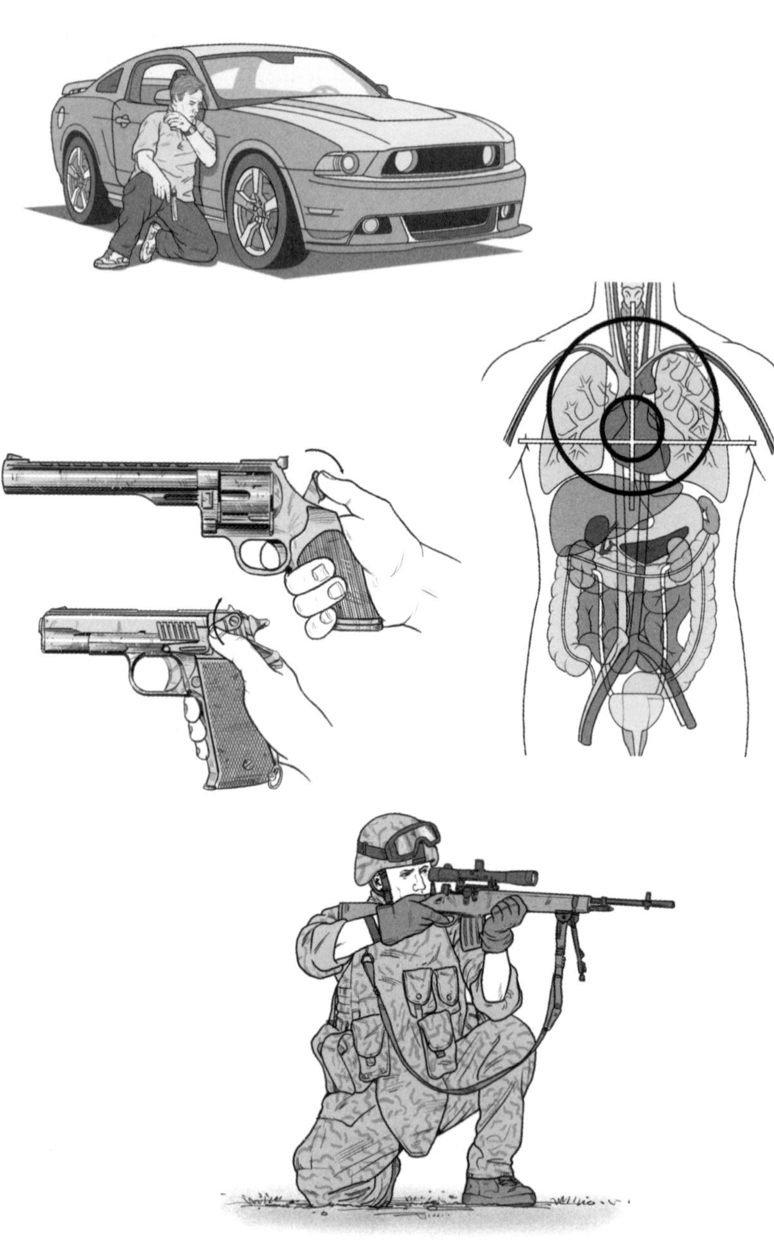

Guns are perhaps the most dangerous of all handheld weapons and should be handled and dealt with carefully.

Firearms

Firearms are projectile weapons – they launch a small, dense object at high speed along a ballistic trajectory. Bullets can be considered to travel in a straight line over a short distance, but at greater ranges a bullet will 'drop' due to the effects of gravity and may drift off course if there is any wind between the firing point and the target. Long-range shooting is something of an art form, requiring not only good marksmanship but also an ability to estimate atmospheric conditions and the effects of gravity. Such skills are beyond the scope of this book.

At close range, the only factors that really matter are where the weapon is pointing when the trigger is pulled and how fast the target is moving. Between the decision to shoot and pulling the trigger there is a very short delay, followed by another one as the weapon's trigger activates its mechanism and fires the round. This is referred to as 'lock time'. After this, the bullet has to get to the target. At very short range this takes only a split second, but when all three delays are considered it is possible that a rapidly moving target could have

Marksmanship is only one element of effective firearm use. Use of cover and the ability to spot a fleeting target in the midst of a gunfight are also key skills.

Sighting a Moving Target

Shooting directly at a moving target is an exercise in futility at any but the closest of ranges. The target must be 'led' a little to ensure that bullet and target arrive at the same spot simultaneously.

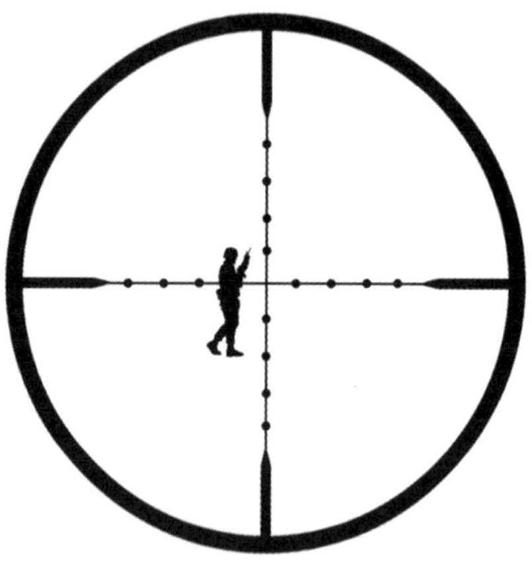

travelled some distance out of the line of fire or into hard cover.

Moving Targets

When shooting at a moving object it is necessary to 'lead' the target so that the bullet and target arrive at the same point at the same time. A faster target requires more lead, and at greater ranges more lead is also required as the projectile will take longer to reach the aim point. However, by far the greatest cause of inaccuracy is the weapon user. Under the stress of combat many shooters will yank the trigger instead of squeezing it evenly, which can jerk the weapon off target. Failure to control recoil can also cause shots to miss, especially during very rapid shooting if the user does not get the weapon properly back on target before firing the next round.

A good, solid stance with the weapon firmly held in both hands helps reduce inaccuracy, partly by controlling recoil and partly by eliminating variables. If the weapon

Solid Shooting Position

A solid shooting position gives a constant relationship between the shooter's eye and his weapon, and allows him to make best use of his marksmanship skills.

is always the same distance from the user's eye and his body is always aligned the same way then shooting will produce consistent results. Practice allows the shooter to place the area he can consistently hit over any target that appears – for example if a shooter learns to create a small 'group' when shooting but consistently shoots down and right from the aim point, he can train himself to correct this. The key is to create the capability to consistently put shots into a small area, then learn to move that area to where it is wanted.

Wherever possible, a trained shooter will use one of several well-proven firing stances. He will turn his whole body to engage a target that appears to the side, rather than attempting to point the weapon using just his arms. Waving weapons around like this or worse, turning them sideways 'gangsta' fashion, simply leads to wasted ammunition and quite possibly second prize in a fight to the death.

Instinctive Shooting

At close range, accurate shooting is more or less instinctive. The shooter looks at the point where he wants his rounds to go and puts the front sight of the weapon over it, usually using binocular vision. The back sight is irrelevant at such a short distance. This sounds simple but most people cannot shoot accurately even at close range, and once the stress of combat takes hold, even a good marksman can become erratic. Gunfights often take place at ridiculously short ranges and result in few or no hits. This is sometimes due to incompetence but more often it is simply because hitting a target is much more difficult than Hollywood normally makes it appear.

Bullets are propelled by expanding gases that are created by the rapid

Aim Point

The correlation between sight alignment and bullet strike is indicated below. The upper line represents a telescopic sight with standard crosshairs, while the lower row represents a front blade sight.

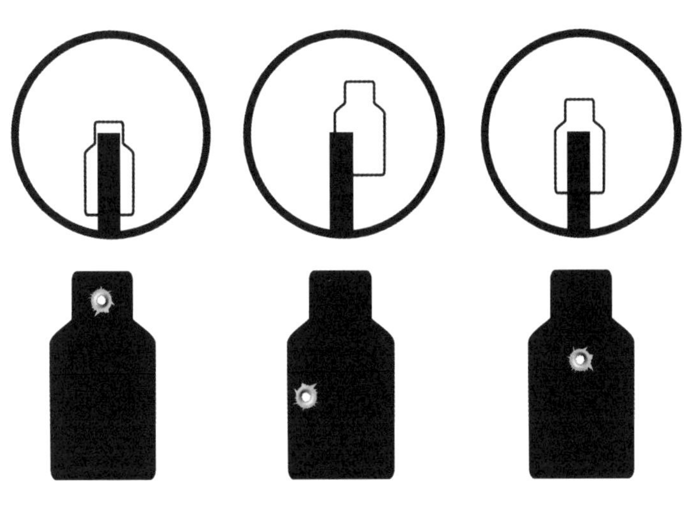

combustion of propellant held within the cartridge. This takes place in a firing chamber, and drives the bullet out of the weapon down the barrel. Some of the propellant gas also comes out of the barrel, causing muzzle flash and a great deal of noise. Weapons can become hot when fired; anyone training to defend against guns at close range must be prepared for this. Flinching at the noise of a discharge or letting go of a hot gun is likely to lead to being shot by the next round.

Firing is initiated by the trigger mechanism, which does not directly fire the bullet. In most weapons, a spring-loaded hammer is held ready to 'fall' when the weapon is cocked. The trigger simply removes an obstacle from the hammer's path and allows it to fall. This requires very little effort, allowing the weapon to be fired with a small pressure of the finger.

The hammer usually falls onto a pin or striker, which in turn is driven into the cartridge with some force. At the rear of the cartridge (on the rim in some weapons, in the centre on most) is a primer, a small explosive device that detonates when struck. This in turn initiates the main charge. The propellant creates a large amount of rapidly expanding gas in the chamber, behind the bullet. Unable to escape in any direction except by pushing the bullet down the barrel, this hot

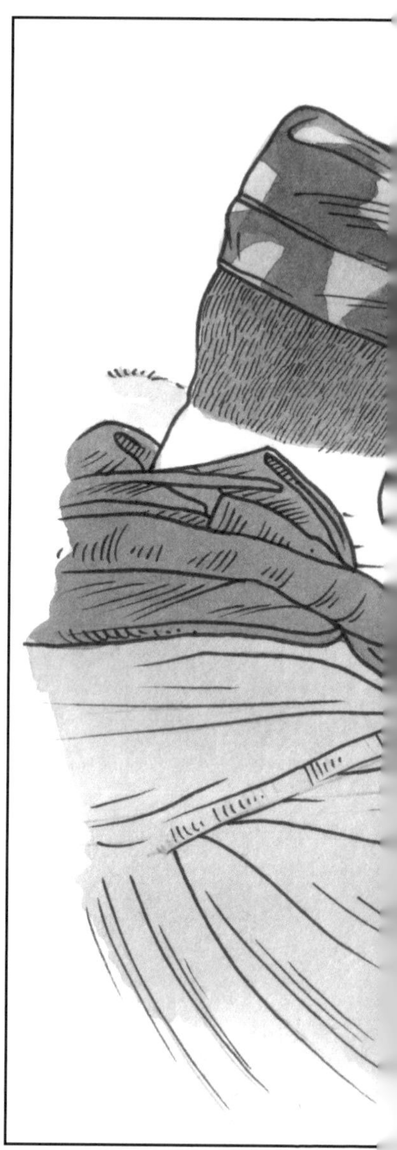

Target Practice

Considerable practice is necessary to become a good marksman. The first stage is to achieve a consistently small 'group' of hits, then to learn to put the group where you want it to be.

Sporting Guns

Sporting guns tend to have a very limited ammunition supply and usually have a manual action or require reloading after each shot. They can be deadly but are of limited combat effectiveness when compared to military systems.

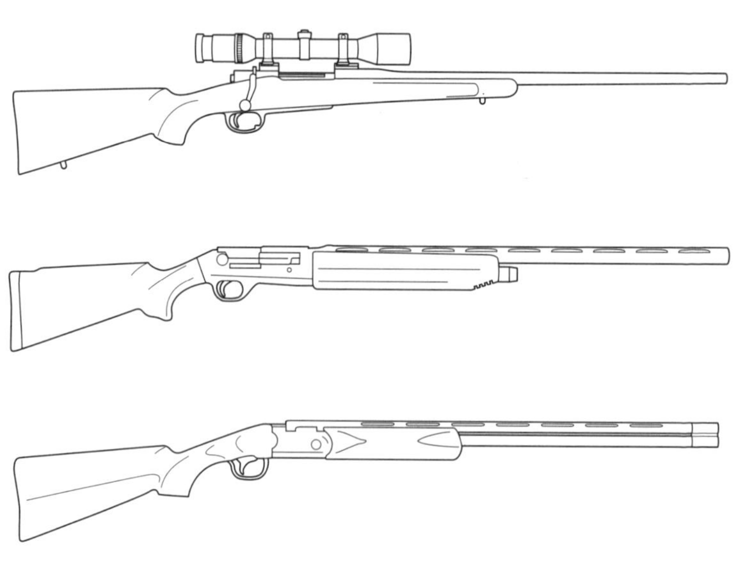

gas is what sends the bullet on its way.

The bullet is the part of the ammunition that leaves the barrel of the weapon and the cartridge (or cartridge case) is the casing that holds the primer, propellant and bullet. The term 'cartridge' or 'round' can also be applied to the whole piece of ammunition. In virtually all firearms the bullet is fired from the weapon but the cartridge case is left behind and must be removed from the firing chamber before the weapon can be reloaded. How this is done is a major factor in defining the type and characteristics of any firearm.

Types of Firearm

There are several basic classes of firearm, with many subdivisions. The lines between types are blurred in places, with the method of use rather than weapon calibre or size usually being the determining factor. The feed mechanism, i.e. how the weapon gets its ammunition into the firing chamber, is an important factor in determining its usefulness in close combat.

Single Shot weapons include some target pistols but a more commonly encountered example is the sporting or hunting shotgun. The weapon shoots once and then must be reloaded. Many shotguns are double barrelled either in an over-and-under or side-by-side configuration. This gives two shots, one from each barrel, but the weapon is still a 'single shot' type as each chamber must be reloaded after firing.

Mechanical Repeaters rely on some action by the user to eject a spent cartridge and to chamber or ready the next. In the case of a revolver, the weapon normally holds six rounds (some revolvers have more or less), each in its own firing chamber, which is moved into alignment in turn.

A revolver rotates the next round into firing position each time the weapon is cocked. With most revolvers this can be accomplished by either manually cocking the weapon or by pulling the trigger. The first part of the trigger pull rotates the cylinder and cocks the weapon; the final movement fires it. In the event of a misfire, pulling the trigger again brings a new round into position, so a revolver that has failed to fire remains a threat.

Similar comments apply to mechanical repeaters like pump-action shotguns and bolt-action rifles; working the action will eject a failed round and make a new one ready, so unless the user is prevented from doing this, a 'dud' round is not likely to put the weapon out of action.

Bolt-action, lever-action and pump-action weapons are normally fed from a magazine, which may be internal or detachable. Spent cartridges are ejected from the weapon and a new round loaded by manually working the action.

Semi-Automatic Weapons use the energy of firing a round to work a bolt or slide which ejects the spent cartridge and allows the next one to be pushed into the firing chamber from a spring-loaded magazine. Magazines are normally detachable, allowing for fast reloading. The weapon will fire once for every pull of the trigger and automatically recocks itself ready to shoot again next time the trigger is

Assault Rifle

The AK-47 and its many variants is a selective fire, gas-operated assault rifle capable of fully automatic or semi-automatic fire. It is effective at both long and short ranges. The simplicity of the weapon's design and operation has meant that it is the most widely produced and copied assault rifle in history.

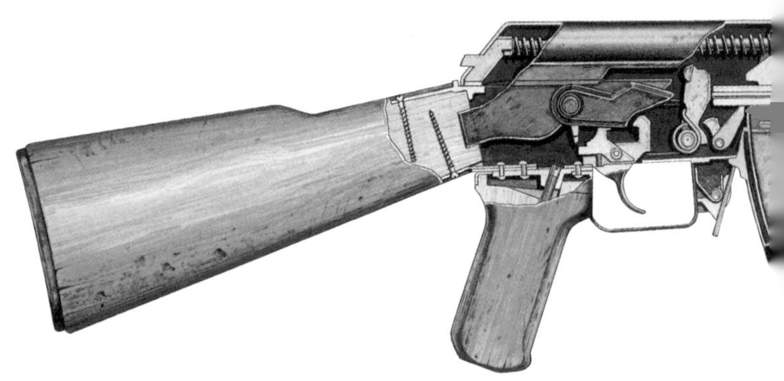

pulled. Generally speaking, a semi-automatic weapon can shoot much faster than a mechanical repeater.

Fully Automatic Weapons work in a similar manner to semi-automatics, but if the trigger is held they will continue to chamber and fire rounds until the magazine is empty. This makes automatic weapons extremely dangerous at close range as they can deliver multiple hits or else be hosepiped onto the target, greatly increasing the chance of being shot.

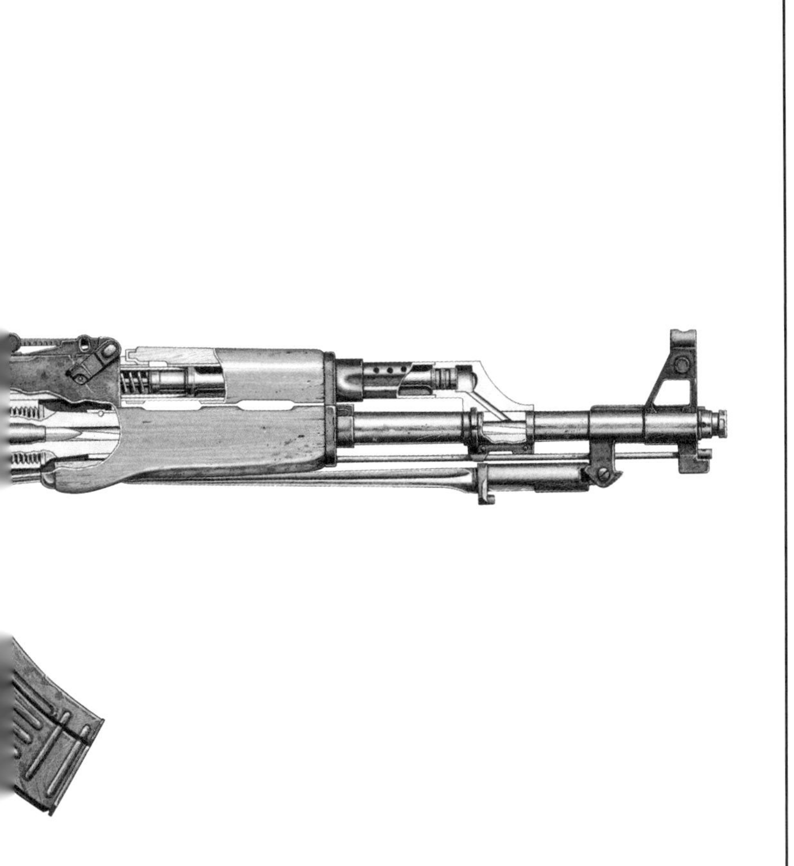

Burst-capable weapons use the same principle but have a device to cut off the firing mechanism after so many rounds (often three), firing a burst for every pull of the trigger.

Most military firearms are semi-automatic or fully automatic, relying on firing one round to chamber the next. This means that, under most circumstances, pulling the trigger again if the weapon has failed to fire will not cause it to discharge. If the problem is merely a 'dud' round, it can be ejected by manually

Semi-automatic Handgun

Most 'combat handguns' are semi-automatic designs that can be quickly reloaded in action. Although their effective range is limited, semi-automatics offer a good balance of firepower and ease of carry.

working the charging handle and the weapon will then be ready to fire (again, assuming that the user is not prevented from doing so). In some cases, however, a fully or semi-automatic weapon that has failed to fire will be thoroughly jammed and require anything from a few seconds' work to a major disassembly to get the jammed round out.

In addition to the feed mechanism, the general characteristics of the weapon will dictate how and when it is used.

Handguns are small weapons intended to be used in one or both hands, and are generally carried as backup weapons or by personnel who are not expecting to have to fight in the immediate future. Most military handguns are semi-automatic but revolvers remain popular for private use, largely for their simplicity. Handguns use a relatively short cartridge, which reduces their ability to penetrate cover or body armour, but can still deliver serious wounds. The short barrel of a handgun affects accuracy, and their effective range is

Double-barrelled Shotgun

Many sporting shotguns are double-barrelled designs reloaded by breaking open the weapon and placing new cartridges into the breech. This is a much slower process than changing a magazine.

much shorter than most people imagine.

Shotguns are smoothbore weapons (i.e. they are not rifled to spin the projectile for stability) that can fire a single solid projectile but normally use a number of smaller pellets. The effective range of a shotgun is fairly short and they lack penetrative power, but at close range their stopping power is unparalleled. The shot travels outward in a cone shape that increases the chances of a hit at moderate ranges and ensures that several pellets will hit the target at close range.

Many civilian shotguns are single or double-barrelled single shot weapons, but combat shotguns tend to be pump-action or sometimes semi-automatic weapons. It is common for combat shotguns to be fed from an internal magazine

Light Automatic Weapons

Submachine guns and Personal Defence Weapons (PDWs) are ideal for close-range urban combat. They deliver high firepower out to a modest effective range, which is entirely enough for most purposes, but are outranged by rifles in open terrain.

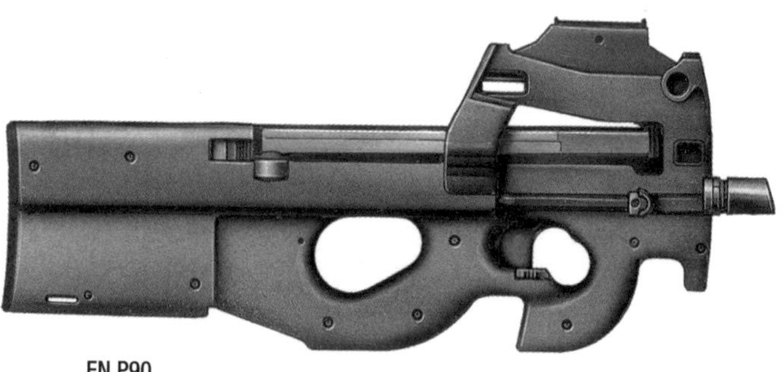

FN P90

that is manually reloaded one shell at a time. This is a relatively slow process. Some combat shotguns use a detachable box or even a drum magazine, and there are a few fully automatic 'assault shotguns' on the market.

Submachine Guns and Personal Defence Weapons are small, fully automatic firearms normally chambered for pistol-type ammunition. They are short, light and handy, and ideally suited to close combat in an urban environment. Almost all light automatic weapons of this sort use detachable magazines, so can be reloaded very quickly. They are designed to deliver high firepower at short range, and in general lose accuracy at longer distances.

Rifles are full-sized weapons firing a longer cartridge than pistols or

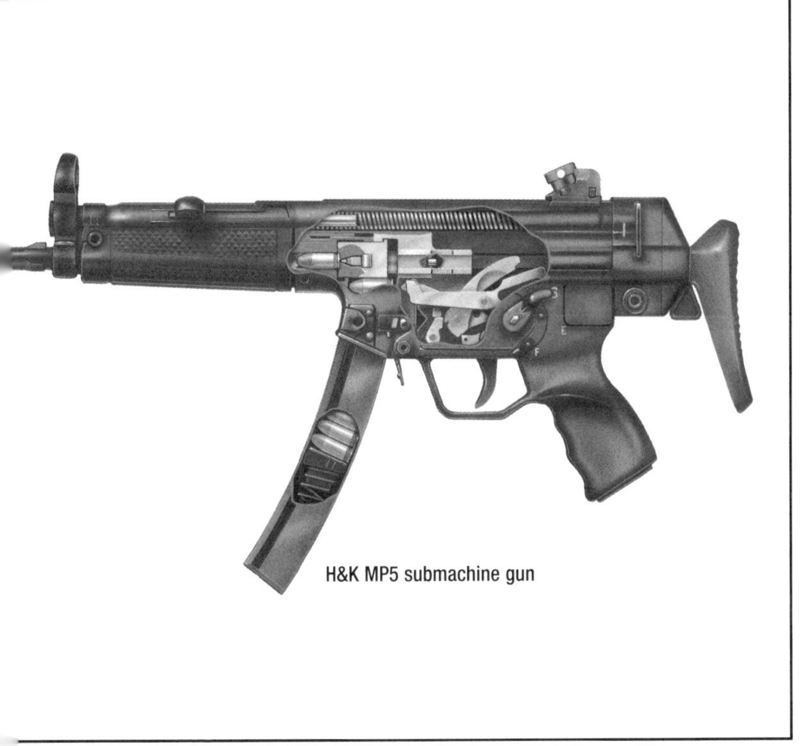

H&K MP5 submachine gun

Bolt-action Rifle

Many sniper weapons and most civilian hunting weapons are bolt-action designs. After each shot the bolt is manually operated, ejecting the spend case and loading a new round. This results in a fairly low rate of fire, which is offset by the weapon's accuracy at longer ranges.

submachine guns, which gives them greater penetration, accuracy and wounding power. Rifles range from bolt-action hunting weapons to fully automatic assault rifles capable of firing as fast as a submachine gun. The effective range of a rifle is generally further than most users can shoot accurately, and a rifleman can therefore be considered a threat to anyone he can see. Most military rifles are fed from detachable magazines while civilian weapons may have a small detachable magazine but more commonly use an internal one. Carbines are essentially smaller and lighter versions of a rifle, and for close-combat purposes they perform more or less the same, other than being lighter and handier in confined spaces.

Safety Devices

Most firearms have some kind of safety device to prevent an accidental discharge. Revolvers

M40A1 rifle

tend not to have a manual safety catch, relying on an internal device that prevents the weapon from discharging unless the trigger is pulled. The assumption, not unreasonably, is that if you pull the trigger, then you want to shoot something. Many modern semi-automatic pistols also have no manual safety device but use grip or trigger safeties. Again, if the weapon is held properly and the trigger is pulled the weapon will discharge. When and where that happens is the responsibility of the user.

Manual safety catches are common on many semi-automatic pistols and most other firearms. In the case of fully automatic or burst-capable weapons the selector is also the safety catch, allowing the user to determine whether the weapon fires one shot, many shots or no shots at all each time the trigger is pulled.

Many firearms have other controls too, which might include a magazine

Handgun Safety Devices

Many semi-automatics (below) have a manual safety device that prevents the weapon firing until it is disengaged. Thus it is safe to carry most semi-automatics 'cocked and locked', but a cocked revolver is something of a hazard to all concerned.

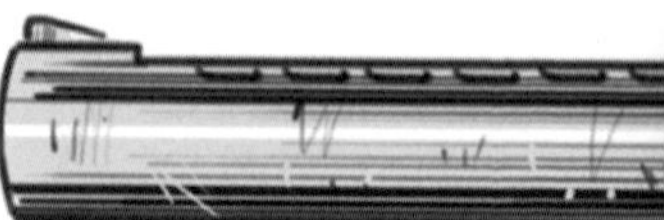

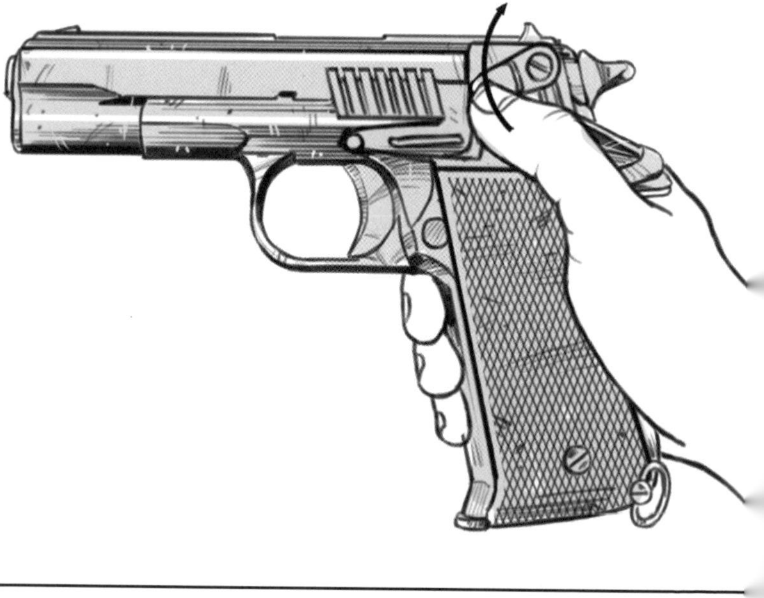

Most revolvers (above) have no manual safety devices, but they do have a device that prevents the hammer from contacting the firing pin unless the weapon is cocked – either manually as shown here or by pulling the trigger for a double-action shot.

Spring-loaded Slide

Semi-automatic handguns use recoil energy to drive the slide back, opening the ejection port and throwing out the spent cartridge case. The spring-loaded slide then runs forward, picking up a round from the magazine and chambering it. The action of the slide also cocks the hammer, readying the weapon to fire again.

release and/or decocking lever. An untrained person who grabs an unfamiliar weapon may not be able to get it to work in time to be useful even if it is loaded and a round chambered. For this reason many close-combat experts advocate not trying to shoot with any weapon you are not familiar with. If one is grabbed from an opponent, get it out of the equation by throwing it far away or under something, then disable the opponent by other means. For those with the training, of course, an opponent's weapon may be the key to victory.

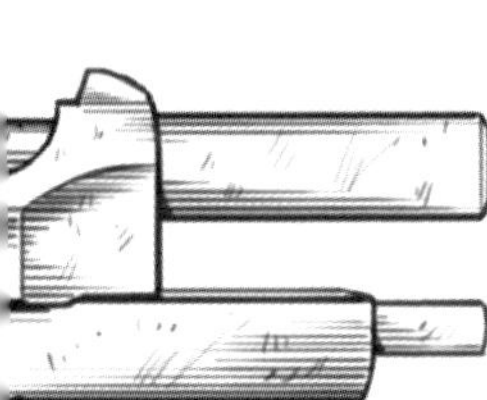

Handguns at Close Range

Whenever possible, handgun users will try to assume a good two-handed firing stance. The weapon is held in both hands, creating a push-pull lock (front hand pulls back, rear hand pushes forward). The weapon's muzzle is pushed towards the target as if the user were trying to stab it with an infinitely long bayonet on the front. Aiming is normally done with both eyes open, simply placing the foresight over the target.

The shooter will stand weak-side-forward, knees slightly bent, and lean into the weapon. It is possible to move quite quickly in this posture, though it can be tiring. Movement is as smooth as possible, but shooting when moving at all is never very accurate.

Taking Cover

If the shooter has any choice at all in the matter, he will normally take cover and rest the weapon on something solid. The hand position remains much the same as the shooter crouches or kneels behind any object that might offer some cover or concealment. This is not always possible, and often it is more imperative to engage the target immediately than to look around for something to hide behind. In this case, a fast knockdown is the best defence, and forcing the opponent under cover with near misses comes a good second.

Even when firing from a good stance, most shots will miss. There are times when it is appropriate to empty the weapon as fast as possible, but for the most part trained shooters will fire two shots

Two-handed Firing Stance

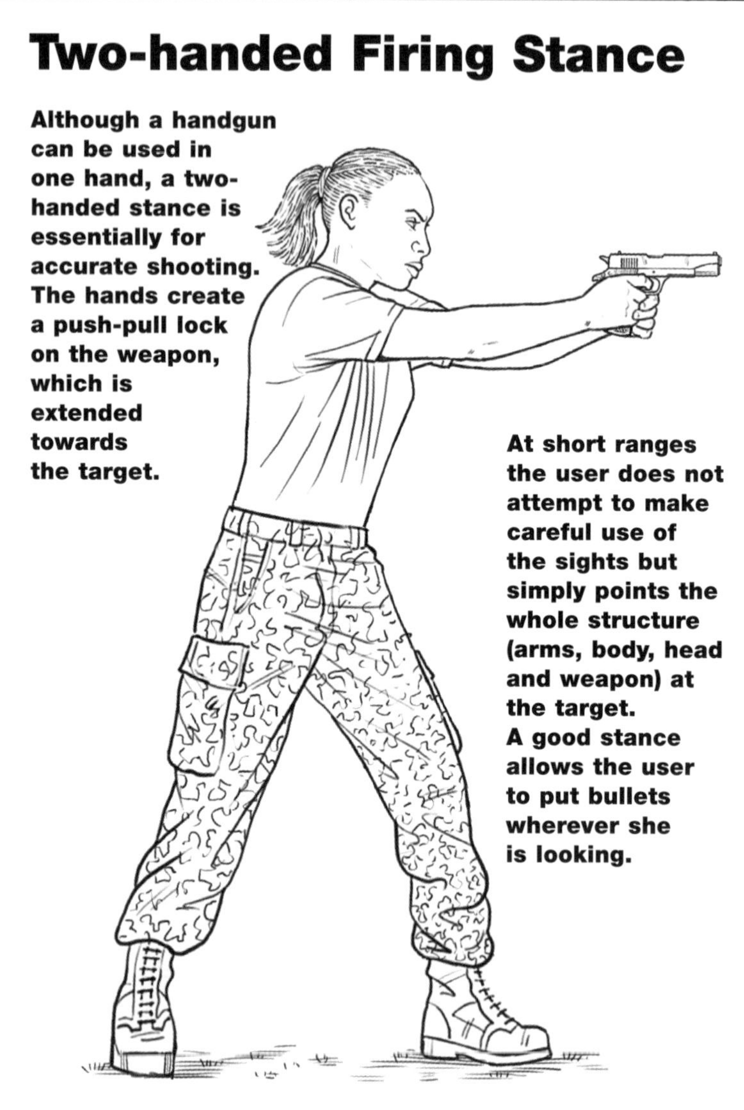
Although a handgun can be used in one hand, a two-handed stance is essentially for accurate shooting. The hands create a push-pull lock on the weapon, which is extended towards the target.
At short ranges the user does not attempt to make careful use of the sights but simply points the whole structure (arms, body, head and weapon) at the target.
A good stance allows the user to put bullets wherever she is looking.

in rapid succession, known as a double-tap, then aim again and fire another.

If the weapon has to be drawn or deployed after combat has begun, then it will need to be readied. Many modern semi-automatic pistols and almost all revolvers have a double-action trigger, which means that providing there is a round in the firing chamber, the weapon can be brought into action simply by pulling the trigger. The manual safety catch, if there is one, must be disengaged first.

Condition One

Many users of more traditional semi-automatic pistols carry their weapon 'condition one' or 'cocked and locked', i.e. with a round chambered and the hammer cocked but the safety on. A weapon that is 'condition two' has a round chambered and the safety on, but the hammer uncocked. Not all

Taking Cover

Use of cover and concealment are essential to surviving a firefight. A car offers only concealment for the most part. Only the engine block is solid enough to stop a bullet reliably.

Kneeling Firing Stance

A kneeling stance allows the shooter to support the weapon and keep it stable. As a general rule the more points of contact there are with the ground and the lower the stance, the more accurate the shooter will be.

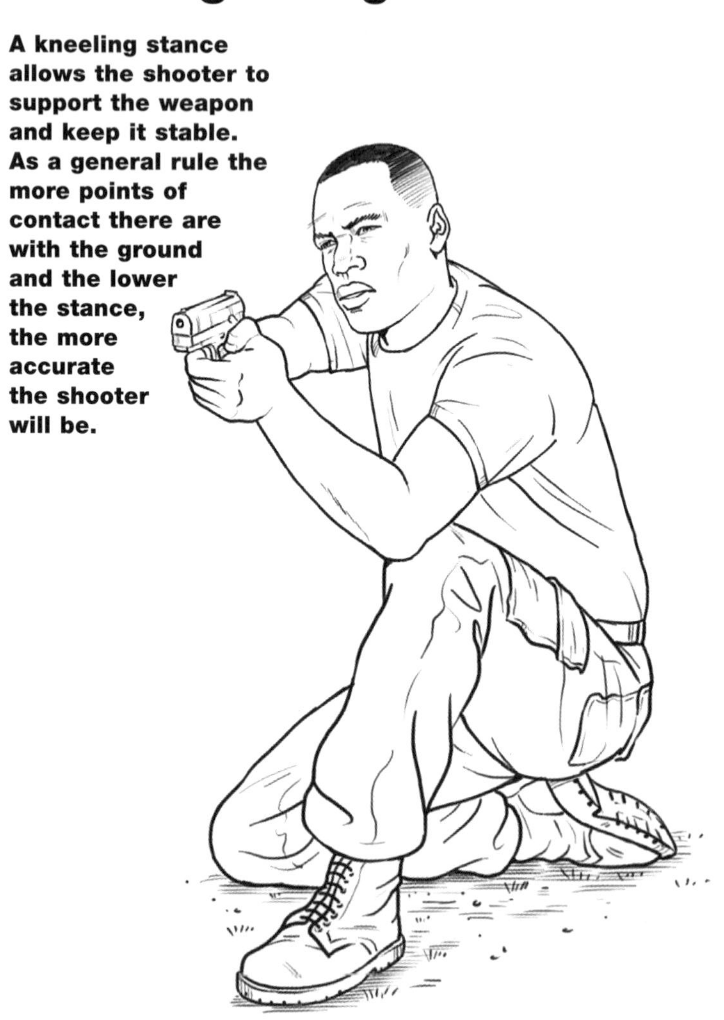

semi-automatics are safe in this condition; almost all modern weapons are but many older designs can discharge if the hammer is bashed against something by accident.

With a weapon that is condition one or two, readying it is a matter of taking the safety off and cocking the hammer if necessary. There is no need to work the slide as there is a round already chambered. 'Condition three' means that the hammer is uncocked and there is no round in the chamber. A weapon in this condition cannot discharge, accidentally or otherwise, unless a round is chambered and the hammer cocked. This is achieved by pulling the slide all the way to the rear and allowing it to run forward again.

Reloading a semi-automatic weapon in combat is very quick. The user releases the magazine and lets it drop out (or pulls it if necessary), and pushes in a full one through the handgrip. This is an instinctive movement, and is easy to accomplish even in the dark, as one hand can easily find the other. A round is then chambered and the weapon is once again ready to fire. It may be necessary to work the slide to chamber the top round, though some semi-automatics have a slide lock that holds it open when the weapon is empty. A catch on the side releases the slide and allows it to run forward to chamber the round, completing the reloading process a little quicker.

Loading a Revolver

A revolver is slower to load, especially if each round must be chambered manually. A speedloader or similar device can make the

Condition Zero

Nobody in their right mind carries a gun 'condition zero' – with a round chambered, hammer cocked and the safety catch off – unless it is designed to be safe in this mode. A weapon that is condition zero is ready to shoot with just a slight pressure on the trigger. That's fine in combat but not so good in the waistband of your jeans.

Loading a Revolver

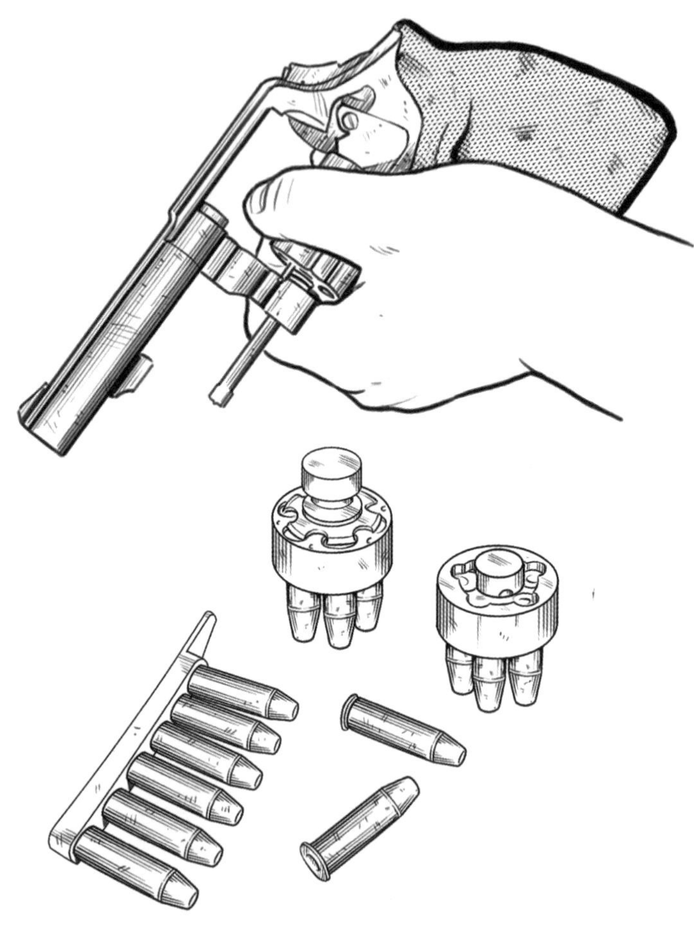

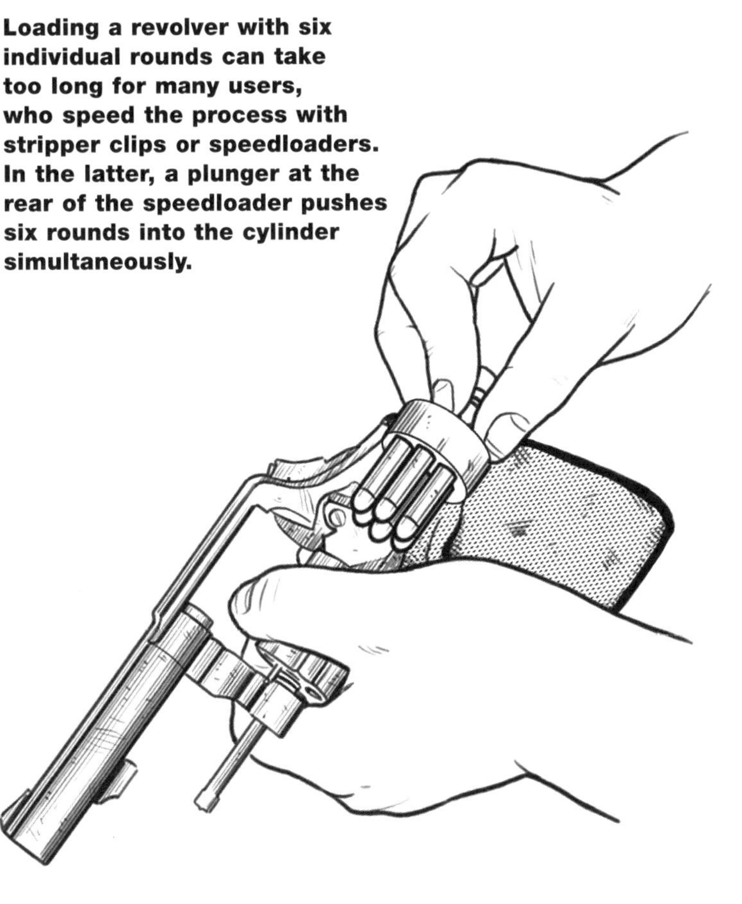

Loading a revolver with six individual rounds can take too long for many users, who speed the process with stripper clips or speedloaders. In the latter, a plunger at the rear of the speedloader pushes six rounds into the cylinder simultaneously.

process faster by inserting several rounds at once, but this is still slower than reloading a semi-automatic weapon.

Conversely, it is sometimes necessary to make safe a weapon grabbed from an opponent during a fight. A revolver can be made safe by pushing the cylinder release, swinging it out and ejecting all the rounds by pushing the ejector rod. A semi-automatic is made safe by removing the magazine and then working the slide at least once to eject any round in the chamber. A potentially fatal mistake is to work the slide and then eject the magazine, leaving the weapon cocked with a round in the chamber.

Very small automatic firearms (small submachine guns and some personal defence weapons) are often used in a similar manner to handguns as they resemble these more than they do full-sized combat weapons.

Draw and Shoot

A drill that remains popular today for less well-trained semi-automatic shooters is to carry the weapon condition three (uncocked, no round chambered, magazine in place and the safety off). When combat starts, the user draws the weapon with the dominant hand and pushes the muzzle towards the target, works the slide with the weak hand and then wraps the weak hand around the dominant hand to adopt a shooting stance.

This system was developed for the Shanghai Municipal Police in the 1930s, operating with very little training in what was then the most lawless place on Earth. While not the most efficient way to use a semi-automatic pistol, this system is reasonably foolproof. Many users who grab a semi-automatic that is not their own in the middle of a fight will use a similar drill, working the slide to chamber a round before trying to shoot. If one is already chambered, then it will be lost, but another will be loaded, so this is a better option than trying to shoot and finding that there is no round chambered or the hammer is not cocked.

If the slide does not need to be operated, the shooter's weak hand normally reaches the shooting position first, and the dominant hand, holding the weapon, is brought to it.

Extreme Close Quarters Draw and Shoot

At extreme close quarters, the user may use the lead (weak) hand to fend off an opponent or push them away, with his hand high on the opponent's chest, while the dominant hand brings up the weapon to a little above hip height to shoot. The aim point must be well below the shooter's outstretched hand.

Chambering a Round

Working the slide of a semi-automatic handgun chambers a round (replacing one that might already be in the chamber) and cocks the hammer. The finger is kept off the trigger until the user is ready to shoot. With the weapon ready and both hands firmly gripping it, a little pressure will send the round on its way.

Longarms at Close Range

The term 'longarm' applies to any firearm intended to be used in both hands, such as a shotgun, rifle, carbine, submachine gun or even many light machine guns. Longarms can be fired from the shoulder, using the sights, or from the hip. The latter is not in any way accurate but allows fast instinctive shooting at extremely close quarters.

Trained personnel operating in an environment where short-range action is likely tend to move with their weapon already at the shoulder, lowering the barrel to reduce fatigue and to make it easier to move in confined spaces. The weapon can be quickly rocked back up to an aiming position if a threat is detected. It requires far less effort to bring up the muzzle of a weapon that is already in place than to shoulder one that is held in some other posture.

Lowering the muzzle also keeps the weapon from pointing at any allies or noncombatants who may be present. When operating in a group, extreme care is taken never to point a weapon at a friendly, even just to sweep the aim point past him.

Close Quarters

At extreme close quarters, it may be necessary to use the butt of the weapon or a bayonet (if fitted) against a threat that suddenly emerges. It can be difficult to bring a long weapon to bear in a confined space or against an opponent who is rushing in. At greater distances, firepower will usually stop those opponents that are not deterred by the appearance of the firearm. However, much depends on the penetrative and stopping power of the weapon.

Rifles in particular tend to produce through-and-through wounds at close range. That is, the round will often penetrate right though a human body and continue out the other side. If it hits a vital organ, this will still kill the target, but a 'stop' depends largely upon dumping sufficient kinetic energy into the target to cause an immediate stop. This is actually more likely with lower-velocity, fatter bullets such as pistol and submachine gun rounds (which are the same, usually) or with a shotgun shell. The very factors that make rifles effective at medium to long range (high velocity and good penetration) can make them less effective at close quarters.

The usual solution to this problem is more firepower. A single rifle round may not immediately stop the target but a burst usually will. The chances of a hit are also increased when firing a burst, but so is the danger of overpenetration or ricochets. Overpenetration, where a round goes through the target or misses it and punches through a wall, can be a serious hazard

Close Quarters Draw

The soldier creates space to use his weapon by shoving the opponent back with his weak hand. His weapon is kept low to prevent it being grabbed, and also to avoid shooting himself in the hand!

Assault Team

In an assault team, different weapons have different purposes. Shotguns will knock down hostiles fast but are imprecise and perform poorly against armour or cover. Carbines and submachine guns are more precise but may require several rounds to drop a target. Some team members use handguns, leaving a hand free to open doors or drag hostages to safety.

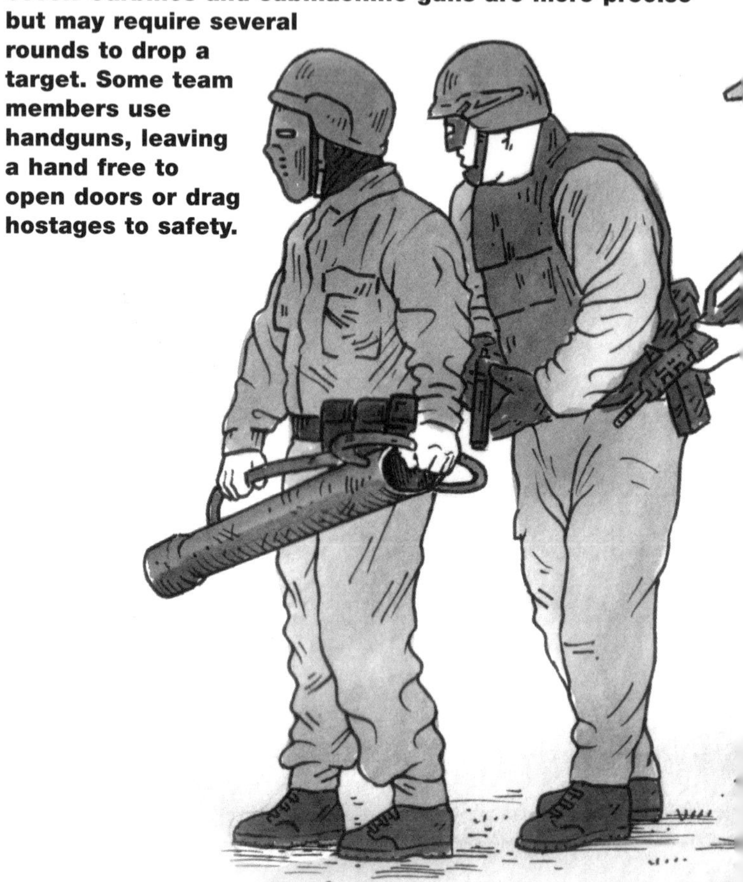

Target Areas

A hit to the heart or its immediate surroundings will often be instantly fatal, but most other areas of the torso will not. Internal bleeding or organ damage can kill fairly quickly, but may not stop a hostile from returning fire or killing a hostage.

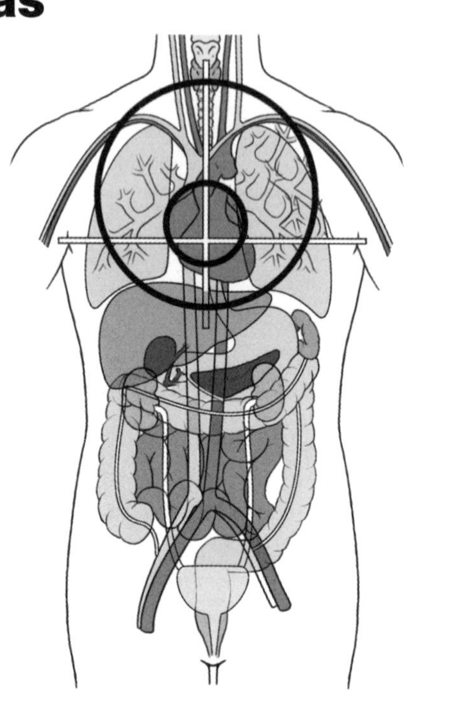

to noncombatants or friendlies who may be out of sight beyond an obstruction.

This is one reason why shotguns and submachine guns are the longarms of choice for hostage-rescue and similar law enforcement teams that operate in an urban environment where members of the public may be nearby. Military personnel tend to use their standard weapons for urban combat, which will typically be assault rifles and light support weapons, as they need all-round combat capability and cannot be as specialized as law-enforcement organizations.

Home Defence and Self-Defence

The primary firearms for home defence are handguns and

When to Deploy

It can be difficult to decide whether or not to deploy a weapon, and personal judgement must be used. The only useful guide is whether or not a credible threat to life exists, or if not using the weapon could result in losing any chance to act later. For example, if armed bank robbers are interested only in grabbing cash then exchanging shots with them may in fact increase the risk to bystanders. On the other hand if they are searching and tying up or brutalizing their captives then there is an element of 'now or never' to the situation. Shooting may still not be a good option... but it might possibly be the only option.

shotguns. Automatic weapons are unlikely to be available to the public, but semi-automatic versions of the same weapon are common in many regions. A rifle might be a good choice for someone who has a fair amount of land and might need to deal with intruders in the open, but most people who own a firearm for home defence will need to consider the implications of shooting indoors or at extremely short range.

Overpenetration is a major issue for home-defence shooters, as their family members might be on the other side of a flimsy partition wall. They may also have to deal with an armed intruder at 3.00 AM, having just woken up. Revolvers are widely favoured for their simplicity, which is a huge asset in such a situation, though semi-automatic pistols are just as easy to use for a properly trained shooter.

Pump-action Shotgun

Shotguns offer a number of advantages – good stopping power, little chance of overpenetration and a reduced need for precise aiming – plus the fact that the weapon itself is quite intimidating. It has been suggested that the sound of a pump-action shotgun chambering a round is one of the most intimidating noises in creation, and will cause many intruders to rapidly withdraw.

For self-defence (in those localities that allow weapons to be carried for this purpose), the common choice is a handgun.

It is not usually legal or physically practical to carry a rifle or shotgun around when on foot, though one might be carried in a vehicle. Self-defence weapons are, on the whole, not what anyone would choose to take into a battle but they do provide a measure of combat capability if an unexpected incident occurs.

Concealed Carry

Military and most law enforcement personnel, of course, carry their weapons openly, but there are occasions where concealment is desirable. Some self-defence users prefer or are required by law to carry their weapons concealed. Small handguns, usually of low power, small calibre and with little ammunition capacity, can be carried in a bag or pocket, or easily concealed about the person. Larger weapons are harder to conceal, though often a jacket will suffice.

Deploying a concealed weapon can take considerably longer than unholstering one that is openly carried, and many users train specifically to get their weapon into play as fast as possible. Good design plays a part here, too – the ideal concealed-carry handgun has few projections to snag clothing as it is drawn.

There are occasions where the best thing to do is, in fact, nothing at all. Having a weapon about your person gives you capabilities, but that does not mean that fighting is the best option, or even a good one. For example, during the 1980 Iranian Embassy siege in London, an armed British police officer was among the hostages. He was unable to deploy his weapon in time to prevent the attack, and subsequently kept it hidden throughout the siege.

Although he could have used his weapon at any time, the officer elected not to. He was massively outgunned by six hostage-takers and would likely have been quickly killed without managing to eliminate enough of the hostiles to alter the situation. Had the need become imminent, for instance if the gunmen had started killing hostages, then the officer would undoubtedly have done all that was possible to prevent this. In the event, he was able to assist the Special Forces rescue team when they assaulted the building. Thus the decision not to start shooting was the correct one in this case.

At this point it can be too late to reach for a weapon. If things are so desperate, however, that you have no other option, the only chance is to cause or wait for some kind of distraction and then act quickly and decisively. Even so, the odds are not good.

Gun Safe

You should keep all your firearms in a purpose-built gun safe like the one shown here. If the safe is operated by keys, make sure you know where those keys are at all times, and always keep them hidden in a secure location. Also make sure your ammunition is stored securely.

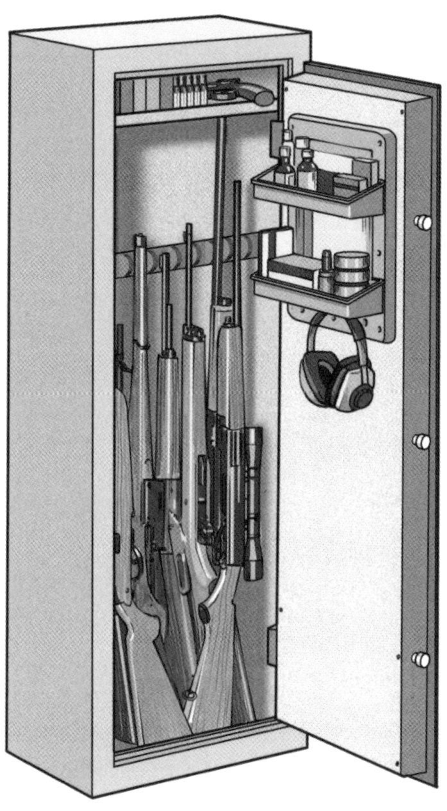

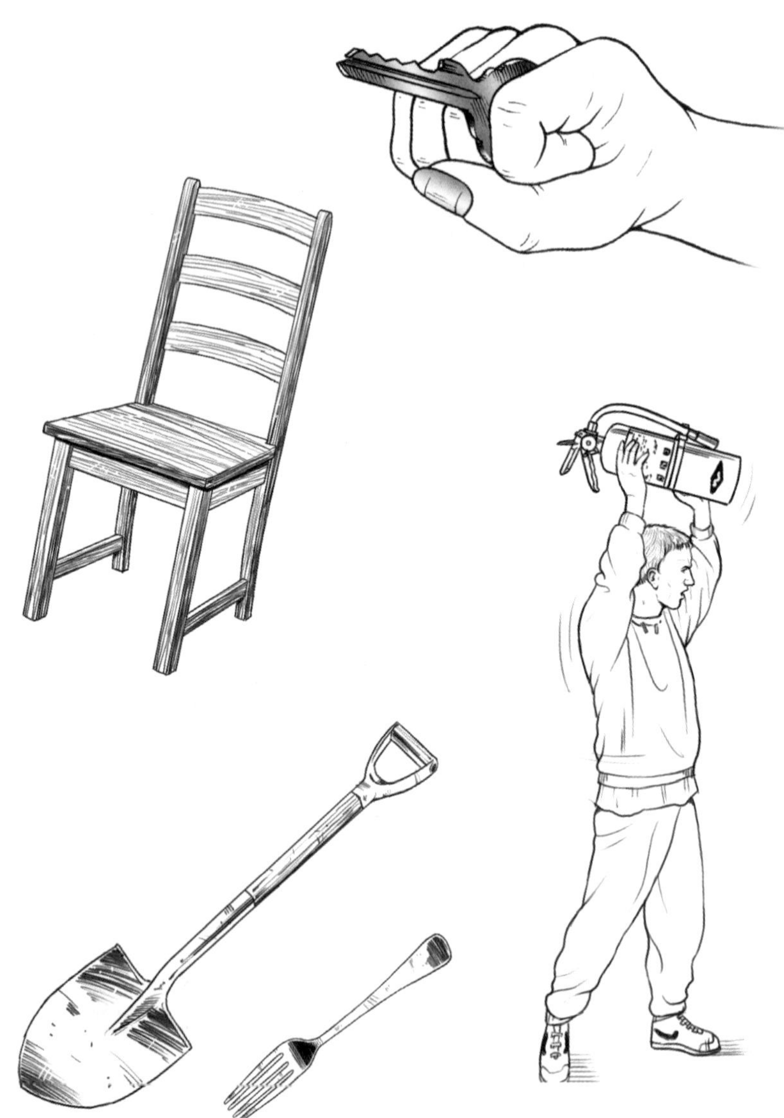

7

Improvised and Miscellaneous Weapons

It is possible to spend a lifetime making a list of the perfect weapon to counter each possible scenario, but the reality is that when violence starts, you fight with what you have.

There are three critical questions when deciding whether or nor to use an improvised weapon. The first is legality. In the case of a civilian under attack, there are laws governing the use of weapons, whether improvised or specifically made for combat. The response to a threat must be proportionate, which means that there are circumstances where using a weapon might result in prosecution. If the threat is severe, such as when the attackers have superior numbers or physical capabilities, or are themselves armed, then the circumstances may justify use of a weapon. If they do not, however, then using one might result in legal entanglements that are best avoided.

Excessive Risk

Assuming weapon use is legal, which it will be in the case of a soldier or law-enforcement officer acting in accordance with his use-of-force training and rules of engagement, then the next question is whether trying to obtain a weapon will expose the defender to excessive risk. For

It has been wisely observed that 'what you're prepared for won't be what happens'. However, there will usually be something nearby that can be improvised as a weapon.

Dealing with a Bayonet Attack

An unarmed defender can evade a bayonet attack by stepping inside the thrust (A). He can then deflect the thrust with one hand, while using his free hand to sieze on any handy implement (B).

The defender can then follow up with a strike to the head (C) before the attacker can bring his weapon to bear once again.

Door Key

Something as simple as a key can be employed as a weapon. The best use is to gouge at an assailant's flesh in order to secure release from a grab. This will not end a situation, but can be followed up or may facilitate escape.

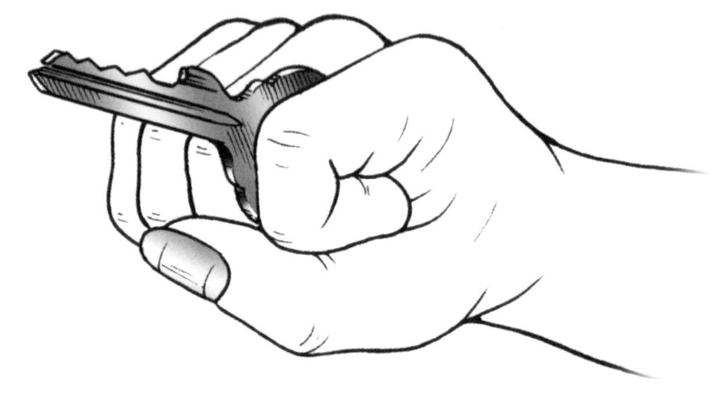

example, if the opponent is very close and launching an attack, then turning away to seek an 'equalizer' will certainly result in being hit. It is better to fight unarmed than to give the opponent a clear shot as you bend down to pick up a weapon.

The final question is one of weapon effectiveness. Some possible improvised weapons are not effective under certain circumstances, or in the hands of some people. A weapon that is too heavy to be used easily is not a good choice. However much damage it might do if it hit the target, if it is too slow due to its weight then it will not be much use.

The opposite is also sometimes the case: some weapons might be a bit too effective. A blunt weapon can be used to deliver non-lethal blows to the arms or legs, but once a sharp or pointed weapon is in play then blood will be drawn.

There are plenty of circumstances where this is entirely appropriate and

Household Implements

Common sense will indicate which household and garden implements can be used as effective weapons. Small and light items are most useful in the same manner as keys – to gouge flesh, inflict pain and secure release from a grab. Larger implements can be used to block as well as strike.

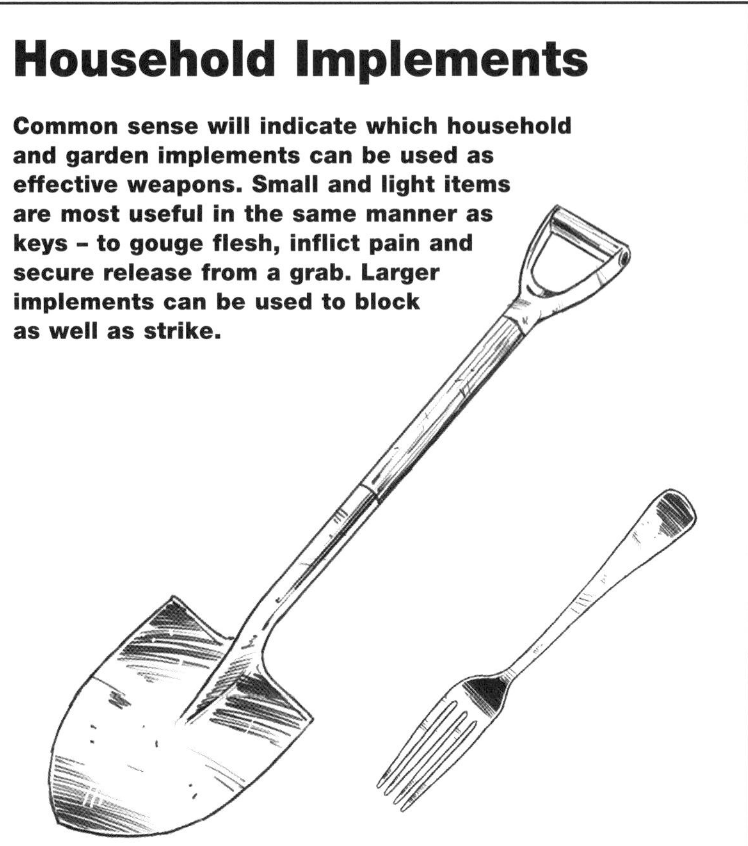

quite legal, but the user must deal with the question of whether or not they are willing to cut or stab an opponent and to deal with the legal and emotional consequences later.

Many improvised weapons parallel other types. For example, a screwdriver can be used like a knife, at least to stab with – it will not cut very well. If an improvised weapon is close to a stick or knife then it can be used in much the same way. Many improvised weapons are different enough to require some thought as to how best they might be used.

Airport Security

People passing through airports are often asked, 'Are you carrying anything that could be used as a weapon?' To be honest, most people are. That is to say, virtually anything can be used to harm another person if you know how and/or try hard enough. However, a lengthy explanation of how your bag strap could be used as a garrotte and your pen could inflict a nasty stabbing wound is not a good idea, however clever it might seem.

For one thing, such an answer might well result in your being arrested or at least refused permission to board an aircraft, and in any case the security personnel are not asking if you have something that could conceivably cause harm; they're really interested in objects designed as a weapon or which could easily be used as one. A pair of scissors makes a pretty decent improvised knife; a plastic pen really does not.

Thus while it is useful to recognize the combat potential of all objects, common sense (and the desire not to be arrested at airports) must apply. Some objects are easily used as weapons; some are very marginal. If airport security do not stop an object being taken on an aircraft, then it is not a good choice as an improvised weapon.

Distraction Tools

Some objects that can be used in combat are not really weapons as such, in that they do little harm to the target. They can be useful in other ways, normally by causing a distraction. The classic example is the 'throw sand in his face' gambit used in countless action movies by desperate heroes or villains who don't fight fair. Kicking up a shower of pebbles or even snow can cause an opponent to flinch if he sees something coming towards his face, while sand or dust in the eyes can temporarily put someone out of the fight.

Any object can serve as a momentary distraction if thrown in the opponent's face. Many self-defence experts advocate carrying a pocketful of loose change for this purpose, but anything will suffice. In the case of a robbery that might be about to 'go bad', the very items being demanded can be used as a distraction. Rather than handing over the wallet or watch (or whatever) the defender tosses it towards the opponent's face and launches a devastating attack while he is momentarily distracted.

This gambit is somewhat desperate if it results in tackling a knife or gun while unarmed, but it might be the only option. Alternatively, it may grant the defender sufficient time to draw his own weapon and bring the situation to a sudden stop.

Rocks and Small Heavy Objects

Most localities, especially outdoors, have numerous small and fairly heavy objects lying around. The most obvious are rocks. A roughly fist-sized rock can be used as a weapon, but the options are actually quite limited. The only useful way to strike with a rock is to drive it downward in a hammering blow, which can still cause injury to the user's hand if the rock is sharp.

A heavy hand-held object might be used to take out a hostile who is attacking a friend by striking them from behind, or to bash a hand, ankle or knee to facilitate escape or release from a grab. Similar comments apply to many other objects, such as food cans, which can be found around the typical home or urban environment, and any other hand-held heavy implements.

It is difficult to strike a decisive blow with a rock against an opponent who can fight back effectively. Such a weapon can be used to strike someone over the head from behind or to add weight to strikes against a downed opponent from a dominant position. These are more commonly 'finishing' moves than 'fighting' techniques, and can result in fatalities from skull fracture. This is not necessarily a problem in the military concept – a soldier who is down to bashing enemies with rocks yet still in the fight is more likely to win a medal than be censured for it – but in terms of civilian self-defence it is problematic.

Someone who gets on top of an opponent and brains them with a rock is unlikely to be able to claim self-defence. Thus these are weapons for desperate combat rather than self-defence. In fact, a better use for rocks and similar objects might be to throw them and either beat a hasty retreat or seek a better weapon.

Large Heavy Objects

Large heavy objects are not ideal for personal combat. Anything that requires massive effort to lift and swing or throw is a poor choice under most circumstances. Apart from anything else, using such a weapon is very tiring and it can be hard to time an attack just right. This means that an opponent might land a counterstrike and still get out of the way of the attack. Blocking incoming blows with a heavy

Fire Extinguisher

A large fire extinguisher is an awkward and heavy weapon that can only be used with fairly large, obvious movements. If an object of this sort is the only weapon available, then you are probably better throwing it at an opponent's chest to send him staggering than trying to strike with it.

I See You Brought Enough for Everyone

Many law enforcement and security personnel dislike working with overzealous colleagues who use incapacitant sprays in the middle of a chaotic melee. With three officers struggling to restrain a violent suspect, the odds of just getting the suspect are slim at best.

implement is virtually impossible, unless it is sufficiently large to simply hide behind.

A heavy object can be clumsily swung or lifted overhead and either part dropped/part thrown a short distance forward or shoved towards the opponent in a horizontal pushing action. Both are relatively easy to avoid but can be highly effective if timed right.

Liquids, Sprays, Powders and Irritants

Liquids, whether hot or otherwise, can be used as a distraction, and some can be deadly weapons. Caustic or very hot liquids can cause burns or blind an opponent, while even less unpleasant fluids can cause eye irritation or respiratory difficulties. Fluids like petrol or lighter fuel will cause irritation and will normally cause a combatant to rapidly shift his priorities from winning the fight to escaping from the situation. The threat of being set on fire, or catching fire as a byproduct of the situation, is a powerful deterrent.

In a fight to the death, using weapons of this sort may be entirely acceptable, but in a self-defence situation the circumstances may not merit such an extreme response. Non-lethal irritants or fluids may, however, be a useful distraction. For example, throwing a cup of hot coffee in someone's face may cause a fairly serious scald or little injury at all, depending on how long the coffee has been cooling, but in either case it will result at the very least in a flinch. This could gain time to grab a weapon, launch an unarmed attack or (probably the best option in many circumstances) make a swift departure from the scene.

Some powders and sprays are also effective improvised weapons. Hosing a fire extinguisher in the direction of an assailant may temporarily render him unable to attack. Different types of extinguisher have different characteristics; breathing in powder will cause at least some coughing and possibly respiratory distress, whereas a water-type extinguisher may be simply unpleasant. All the

Pepper Spray

A can of pepper spray is a useful non-lethal self-defence tool. Spray the contents directly into the face of an attacker, then use their acute discomfort as an opportunity to make a fast escape. If the attacker has a weapon, watch out for him wildly lashing out in panic during his blind state.

same, a jet of water in the face will make the target flinch and the extinguisher will double as a heavy object to strike with.

Blowback

The main problem with any sort of powder or irritant-type weapon is that it can splash or blow back at the user. This is a problem even with the most advanced incapacitant sprays. The latter are carried by law enforcement personnel and are legal for civilians in some regions. They work by projecting a jet of liquid or gas and are aimed at the face. Although their range is short, incapacitant sprays are useful as less-lethal options for security or defensive work.

There are various sprays available. Some use irritant chemicals of the same sort found in tear gas, some are based on capsicum peppers. The chemical irritates the eyes and respiratory system, causing pain and, often, an inability to keep the eyes open. Some people are more or less immune to some agents, and others may suffer greater effects than is common. Although incapacitant sprays are considered 'less lethal' weapons, they can cause fatalities, especially where the target receives a large dose.

The conventional way to use an incapacitant spray is to hold it in the dominant hand, with the weak hand well forward to fend off an opponent and act as a psychological barrier. If possible, a warning is issued and this may be sufficient to deter an opponent or force compliance. If necessary, the spray is directed at the face, and is used when the opponent is beyond arm's length. Spraying someone at close range, or trying to use an incapacitant spray on a suspect who is grappling with a colleague, is likely to result in the wrong people being affected.

Chairs

Chairs are a common improvised weapon, largely due to their ubiquity. This makes them worthy of treatment in their own right. Very heavy chairs are useful only as something to hide behind, but lighter chairs can be effective weapons for those who know how to use them.

Many people will pick up a chair by the back and swing it, or possibly try to swing it by the legs. This is not as effective as the movies might suggest, and in the case of a light folding chair it can lead to disaster if it collapses on the user's arm.

A much more effective way to use a chair is as a combination shield/weapon, with the seat in front of the user, the back down one side and the legs towards the threat. The chair can be angled so that at least some of the legs are pointed at the opponent, and jabbed vigorously at him. It is possible to score hits on the body and head at the same time

Wooden Chair

The humble wooden chair is a useful weapon/shield combination. Rather than swinging it, hold it by the seat with the legs pointed at the opponent and jab sharply. This both keeps him at a distance and inflicts pain that may drive him off.

in this manner, and the opponent can be driven back quite effectively.

Chairs are very much defensive implements when used in this manner. Even a sharp jab to the face is more likely to cause an opponent to break off than to incapacitate him. However, the combination of dealing out pain and being hard to attack can allow a hard-pressed combatant to win enough of a victory to count.

The Small Stick

The 'small stick' was popularized as a martial arts weapon called a Kubotan, but in fact any short length of a heavy and hard substance, too small to be swung as a weapon, will suffice. A pen can be used in this manner, or a typical eating knife that is too blunt to be used to cut with. Such a small implement cannot really do much harm unless the user knows how to make it effective, and is at best a 'force-multiplier' for what are otherwise unarmed combat techniques.

There are essentially three ways to hold the small stick. The most obvious is to grip it around the centre point, with some of the stick protruding from the top and bottom of the hand. Alternatively, a 'knife grip', with the end of the weapon sticking out of the hand in the direction of the thumb, can be used, or an 'icepick grip', with the stick protruding from the bottom of the hand. There are other grips and endless subtleties, but without advanced training many of these are difficult to use.

The small stick can be used to strike with, adding the impact of a solid object to the blow. It is not the weight of the stick that increases effectiveness, but the fact that it does not 'give' in the same way that a hand does. This enables strikes to body parts that would otherwise not be worth hitting.

Small Stick Techniques

The basic small stick blows are a forward jab, much like stabbing with a knife, and a hammerfist-type blow with the base of the hand. Jabs normally target the front torso or the face, but the throat is a valid target if it can be reached. This is more likely to be fatal than a strike to the same area with just a hand. Hammer blows are often directed inwards to the neck or temple area, or the side of the rib cage. A hammering blow to the side of the thigh muscles will often weaken an opponent's leg to the point where he cannot fight or pursue effectively.

Hammer blows can also be used to strike the hands, for example to force a grab to be released. It is not a good idea to try to target hands as they move around, but a grab immobilizes the attacker's hand and makes it easy to hit.

A small stick or similar object can also be used to gouge or apply pressure to an opponent. Anywhere that there is bone close under the skin is a good target that will cause intense pain. This will not end a fight but it may force a release from a grab or choke hold. Keys, pens and other hard objects can be used in the same manner.

Kubotans

Kubotans are often sold as keychain accessories. Despite this alternative use, they are recognized as being weapons first and foremost by the majority of police forces, and are thus illegal in localities where weapons are forbidden. Excuses about novelty key chains or claims that 'it was a present and you didn't know it was a weapon' are unlikely to be accepted.

Broom Handle versus Bayonet

A long stick like a broom handle can be used somewhat like a blunt spear, jabbing at the opponent's face and throat from a distance. Closer in, it can be used to strike with an action similar to paddling a canoe, and to deflect any attempt to hit back.

B
C

Stick Jab

A hard jab into the body will fold the opponent forwards and open him up to a follow-up strike. This could be a swing, but a jab to the head or throat will be just as effective. Indeed, the stick thrust to the neck was taught as a killing move to World War II Commandos.

8

Using a weapon can be effectively combined with 'unarmed' techniques.

'Unarmed' Techniques in Armed Combat

Most people who have a weapon in their hand will most likely forget about all their other options – they are unlikely to kick, headbutt or strike with the unarmed hand. The exception is those armed with knives who will tend to use the unarmed hand to grab and control the target in most cases. Even if the weapon hand has been grabbed and immobilized, most weapon users will struggle to free it rather than hitting with the other hand or driving in a knee strike, even though this might be a more effective method of getting the weapon back in play.

A number of techniques drawn from unarmed combat are highly useful when at close quarters with a weapon. There may be times when getting the opponent's attention by chambering a weapon strike might leave him wide open to a kick to the knee or the groin, and if this works then it is an effective use of the weapon.

Other unarmed techniques can be used to get an opponent on the ground, where he is more easily dealt with, or used to make space to deploy a weapon.

It is easy to think only in terms of the weapon in your hand, but in fact using the weapon may be only one of your options. A kick or grab may catch an opponent out if he expects a weapon strike.

Striking with the Hands

The primary striking tools are closed fists against softer parts of the body, such as the kidney area or solar plexus, and the heel of the palm against harder parts such as the jaw. The edge of the hand and stiff fingers can be used against the throat or side of the neck.

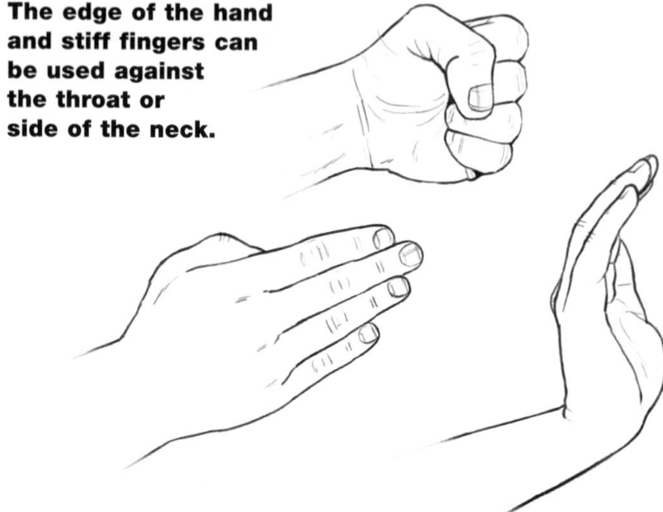

Finally, some unarmed techniques can 'shut down' an opponent, making him shift his attention away from winning the fight and towards dealing with what is happening to him. Shutdown techniques are not fight-enders, but they can shift the initiative in a situation, creating the opportunity to land a telling blow or make an escape from a bad situation.

Pushing Techniques

There are two main pushing techniques: one-handed and two-handed. The mechanics are similar in both cases – instead of leaning on the opponent and pushing steadily, the aim is to deliver a sharp shove, almost like a blow, which will send him reeling and open up a gap. This can be used to deploy a weapon or to make space

A Good Shove

A good shove is a surprisingly useful combat tool. It will create room to kick, strike or draw a weapon. A two-handed shove is directed against the 'creases' of the opponent's shoulders, breaking his posture by tipping his body backwards.

for a good swing, or perhaps to get a weapon positioned to act as a deterrent. An opponent who is shoved away and finds himself looking at a handgun or knife may decide not to come back for more.

Two-handed pushing is only a useful technique if you have both hands free, or if you are holding something quite small. The shove is delivered against the 'creases' of the shoulders, i.e. under the line of the collarbone where the shoulder joint meets the edge of the pectoral muscles.

The push is delivered sharply, with straightening arms, and it is necessary to lunge into it, driving forward with body weight. As the arms snap straight, the opponent should be bent backward slightly, off balance, and driven back a few paces. An opponent who starts moving backwards will eventually stop. If he does not, sooner or later he will disappear from sight and no longer be a threat. If he wants to stay in the fight he will have to start moving forward again, which is an ideal time to hit him. He may, of course, decide not to continue fighting – the space created by a good push can sometimes give an opponent time to realize he does not want to fight on.

A one-handed push is delivered, normally with the weak hand, against the centre of the chest. The sternum or just above it is a good target. A solid push does more than move the opponent back; it also compresses the chest cavity a little, which is a very unpleasant sensation. This can be distracting or demoralizing, making the opponent vulnerable to a follow-up strike or a snarled command to back off. Coupled with the display of a weapon in the other hand, this can be sufficient to end the situation and, if not, the push creates space to use the weapon.

Shutdown Techniques

'Shutdown' techniques include various 'dirty tricks' intended to gain an advantage over the opponent. They only work at

Dirty Tricks

When fighting an opponent who intends you serious harm, it makes sense to employ every dirty trick possible to win the fight. Military combat systems usually include groin kicks, which are delivered with the toes of the boot. There is no need to worry about damage to a foot protected by boots, and the impact is sufficiently powerful that a kick that hits the thigh or abdomen instead of the groin will still damage the opponent.

Groin Kick

Groin strikes are not an automatic fight-ender. More often than not the strike is fairly marginal, hurting the opponent and causing him to pause, but not putting him down. It is necessary to be ready to follow up with additional strikes, or to take the opportunity to flee.

extreme close quarters, but in such a situation they may be more effective than trying to strike an opponent. The aim, when fighting at extreme close quarters is to make enough space to bring your own weapon into play, or to prevent the opponent from doing so. Moving an armed opponent away from you is not always desirable,

Eye Strike

A finger jab to the eyes will not usually end a fight then and there, but it will cause the opponent to flinch and leave him open to whatever you do next. Fingers should be curved slightly downwards rather than stiff, to ensure that they are not broken if you hit the forehead instead of the eyes.

Hand to Face

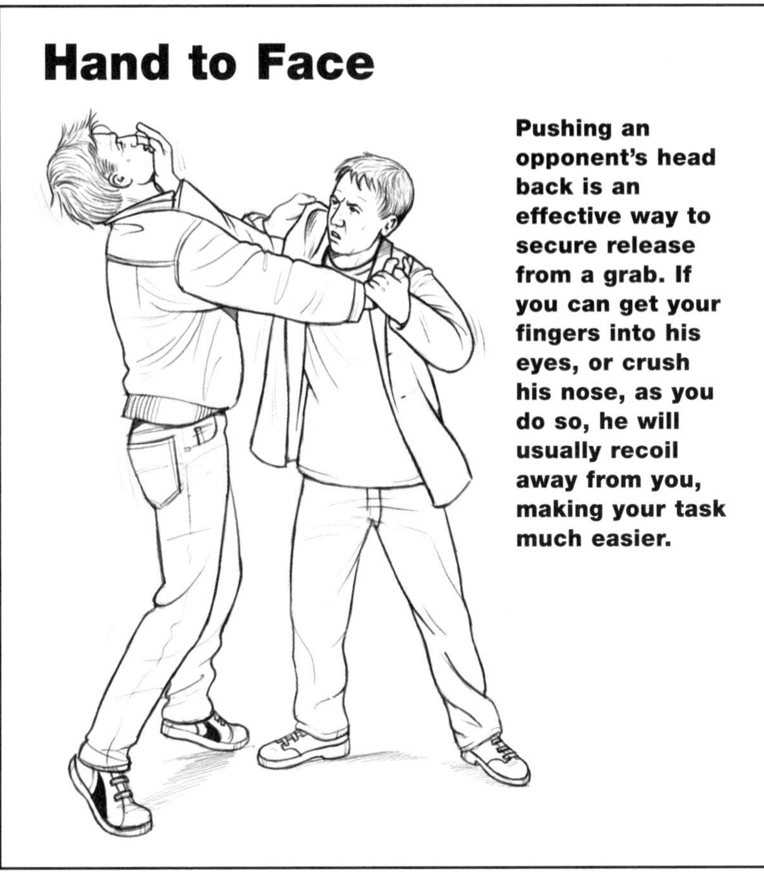

Pushing an opponent's head back is an effective way to secure release from a grab. If you can get your fingers into his eyes, or crush his nose, as you do so, he will usually recoil away from you, making your task much easier.

so rather than making space, a better tactic in this case may be to take his mind off whatever he is trying to do.

Hand In Face

The most basic of shutdown techniques fall under the general heading of 'hand in face'. The weak hand is normally used, but either hand can be effective and, in some cases, other body parts or a weapon can be substituted.

An opponent can be 'peeled off' by placing one hand in his face and pushing his head back, which will

Forearm in Face

A forearm can also be used to strike or push the head back. It can also be used against the throat. The forearm is a useful way to keep the opponent from pushing in – he may be able to push an extended arm to one side but a 'locked' forearm is much harder to dislodge.

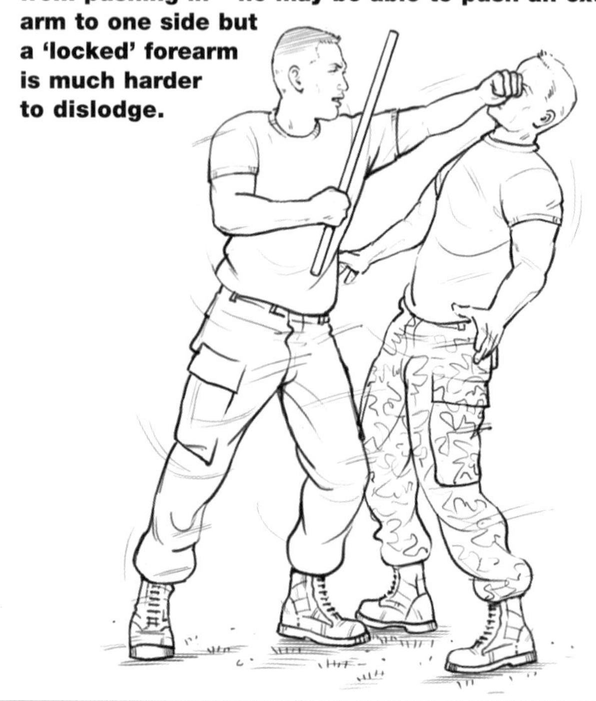

cause his torso to bend backwards. This can secure release from an otherwise tight grip – the opponent may choose to let go because of pressure on his neck, where otherwise his grip might have been too tight to dislodge. He should not be able to bite the hand as it is placed flat over his face.

A less pleasant version of this is to incorporate thumbs or fingers in the eye sockets, or to grab a

Thumb in Eye

The thumb can also be used against the opponent's eye, using the rest of the hand to grip the side of his head. If you miss the eye, dig your thumb in under the cheekbone and press hard.

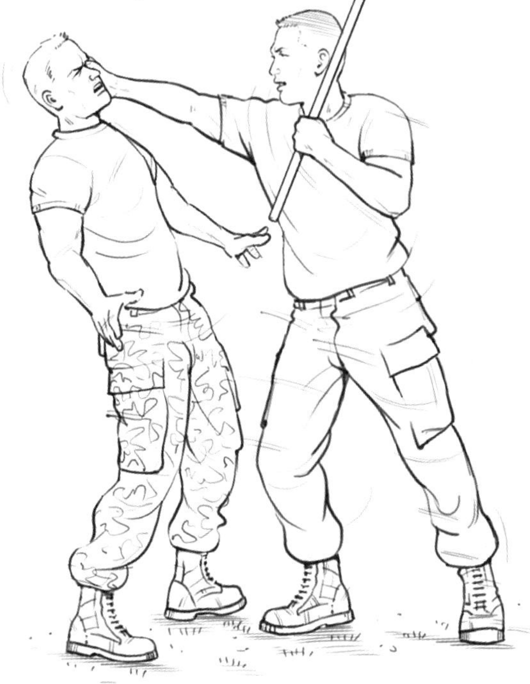

handful of his face and twist at the same time as pushing back. This is deeply unpleasant as well as painful, and most opponents will shift their focus to protecting their face, making the push-back and whatever the weapon hand is doing far more likely to succeed.

Face Bar

The face bar is another good way to shut down an opponent. A face

Bar Choke

A simple bar choke, with the forearm across the throat, is effective if the enemy cannot move backwards. It will work best on the ground with body weight to assist, but is also effective against a wall.

Special Forces Tip: Strike Hard or Not at All

There are no half-measures in armed combat. Avoid conflict if you can, but if you are forced to fight then it is all or nothing. Holding back will get you killed, and possibly others too.

bar is a grappling technique whereby the bones of the forearm are dug into the opponent's face. This is often done as a hold, using the inside of the arm, but the outside of the arm can be used to push his head into the ground or against an obstruction like a wall. A baton or the handle of a weapon can also be used in this manner. The cheekbones and teeth are the best target, ideally with the opponent's head turned to the side. This creates a feeling that bone or teeth are about to break, and will get the opponent's full attention.

Baton Restraint

A baton choke, or 'horizontal vascular restraint' can be locked in by pushing one arm under the baton and then reaching back to grab your own shirt. Pressure on the throat can then be varied by pulling with the other hand or releasing a little.

A forearm or weapon handle across the throat will work in much the same way, choking the opponent and forcing him to fight for release or to move back and open up a space. Chokes with a blunt weapon are extremely effective as there is no 'give'. However, this can lead to unintentional fatalities either due to a crushed windpipe or simply because the weapon user could not feel how much force he was using.

Elbow Strikes

Elbow strikes are excellent close-quarters weapons and can be delivered even if you are holding something. Strikes can be hooked or straight, but need to be delivered with 100 per cent commitment.

Weapon Training Drills

Most weapon-use techniques can be effectively taught by simulating the conditions of the strike or defence in question.

Solo training using a heavy punchbag is effective method up to a point; it is possible to train knife thrusts and slashes on a bag using a blunt weapon, and it is worth doing some stick striking drills with a bag to get the feel for really unloading on the target. Similarly, using targets on a range is the mainstay of firearms training.

For hand-to-hand and close-range weapons training there is no substitute for working with a partner or class. 'Live' weapons should not be used for training. That may seem obvious – only a lunatic would drill gun disarms with a loaded weapon – but stupidity cannot be ruled out, and mistakes do happen. For this reason it is worth ensuring that no live weapons are ever brought into the training area. A live (sharp) knife looks a lot like a blunt training version, and could be picked up by mistake. Robust safety rules are paramount when conducting weapons training; training that puts personnel out of action on a regular basis is not 'hardcore' – it's counterproductive.

That said, realistic training, with weapons that are as close to the real

In combat training, it is necessary to simulate actual combat conditions in order to instil the correct mindset and resistance to the stress of combat.

Baseball Bat Disarm

A forehand swing can be jammed by slamming one forearm into the crook of the elbow and the other into the shoulder. It is necessary to hit hard enough to stop the bat-wielder in his tracks. A takedown is a good follow-up, though knee strikes are another option.

Special Forces Tip: Teamwork

It is always more effective to work as a team than to fight alone, but a group of armed people is not necessarily a team. Getting in each other's way is hazardous at the best of times, but when weapons are involved it can be fatal. Special forces troops do not only train to use their weapons; they train to coordinate their actions with their teammates, to maximize their effectiveness and reduce casualties.

Knife Work

A realistic training knife increases the stress of anti-knife training by making it all feel a bit more real. Training weapons should never be sharp though; training is all about making mistakes and learning from them, and with a sharp weapon involved, any error could be costly.

Trainer's Tip: Knowing What to Do

Combat instructors know that hesitation can be fatal in a fight, and the primary reason for hesitation is not being able to decide what to do. Good combat training teaches fighters to act quickly and almost instinctively – doing something sub-optimal right now is better than standing around trying to figure out the perfect response, or doing the very best thing possible, but too late.

thing as possible is important. A blunt metal knife behaves just like the real thing, and anyone touched by it will know that they could have been cut, on a level that is simply not reached with rubber weapons. Likewise, padded bats and sticks can be used, allowing students to hit each other hard enough to hurt but not cause harm. This makes mistakes less dangerous but ensures that nobody gets complacent.

Most weapons training takes the form of set-pieces – one student makes an attack and their partner performs a defence. This is a good way to learn individual techniques but it can only go so far. At some point it is necessary to introduce more freeform training, much like sparring in boxing. In a more freeform environment, the attacker can do whatever he pleases rather than making an agreed attack, and the defender must react to it however he can.

One way to do this is the 'line up', whereby one student is the defender (armed or otherwise) who is attacked by others in succession. The attackers may have different weapons or may not be armed at all. One useful twist to this drill is to have some of the attackers simply 'posture', shouting threats and making threatening gestures but not actually attacking.

The student must deal with the situation, which may not necessitate weapons use. However, he does not know which of the 'attackers' will suddenly draw a knife or other weapon and wade in.

This sort of scenario-based training is used by police and security personnel, who need to be able to 'read' a situation and act according to the circumstances. In a self-defence context the same drills are useful in order to learn to deal with aggressive behaviour without automatically resorting to weaponry.

Weapon Sparring

In some cases, it is possible to 'spar' with weapons. This can be dangerous and needs close supervision, but a lot can be learnt about weapons use by fighting stick-versus-stick or in a mismatched situation such as stick-versus-knife. Protective equipment such as headguards and body armour should be worn, and contact needs to be kept to a sensible level. This in turn requires a reasonable degree of competence. In a high-stress situation, some students will lose their heads and start swinging as hard as they can. Good training before the sparring begins helps reduce the chances of this.

For extreme close-quarters training, one useful drill is the 'fighting for a weapon' scenario.

Handgun Disarm

Immobilizing the weapon in a position where it cannot shoot the defender is a key element in disarming technique. So long as the weapon stays under control, the defender has a good chance of success.

'Stick Thing'

The 'stick thing' drill starts with both fighters holding the weapon. Whoever gets into a position to use it has won. What happens in between is generally desperate but highly skilled chaos, and is both enlightening and exhausting.

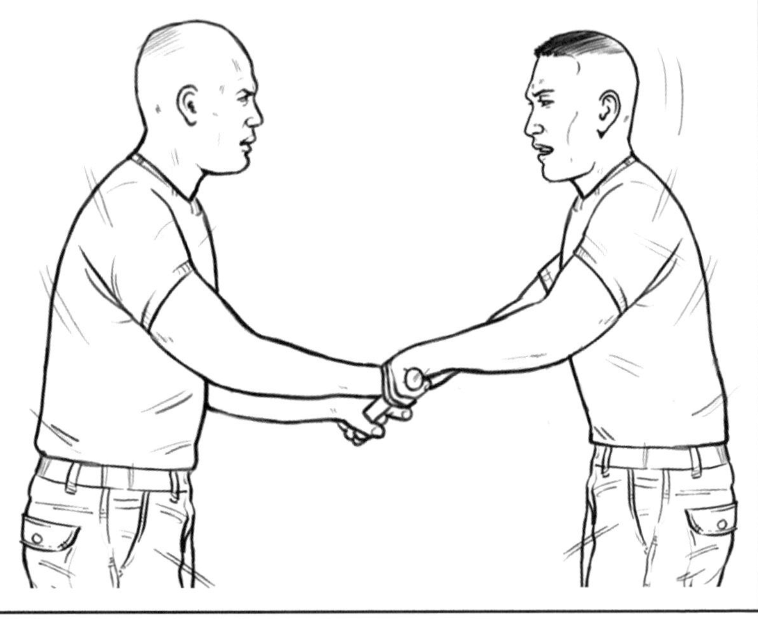

Sometimes referred to as 'the stick thing' for lack of a better name, this drill begins with both students having hold of a stick, using both hands. The winner is whoever gets control of the weapon and simulates landing a telling strike on the opponent.

The 'stick thing' can go on for a very long time, with the students becoming increasingly inventive and devious in their attempts to get control of the weapon. When twisting it, and pulling and pushing do not work, shutdown techniques often come into play. The

Knife Disarm

Against a straight knife thrust the defender deflects the weapon to the side then pivots around to the side. Immobilizing the weapon by wrapping the arm, he strikes the arm to break it. An elbow strike to the back of the head is an effective alternative.

fight may well go to the ground, with one student trying to apply a joint lock or a choke with the weapon in order to make the opponent let go of it.

Variants on this drill, imaginatively referred to as 'the knife thing' and 'the gun thing', are also useful but tend not to go on for so long before someone makes a mistake. Thus the stick thing is the best of these drills for teaching students to keep their head and to look for an effective way to get control of the weapon.

These drills are useful for both self-defence against weapons and for weapon retention training. They are highly competitive and physically as well as mentally demanding, and the results of a mistake are usually very obvious. Though they work best with students who already have some knowledge of close-quarters grappling, they are also beneficial to anyone who expects to use or have to face a weapon at some point.

Tip: Combat Preparation

One useful tool in preparing personnel for combat is the use of 'triggers'. This can be something as simple as shouting 'go!', or can be a physical trigger such as drawing a weapon or assuming a ready stance. The aim is to create a situation where 'if my weapon is in my hand, I'm mentally prepared to use it.'

The choice of whether or not to shoot or strike then becomes a judgement call and is based on necessity, not mental preparedness. A police officer who is killed because he was mentally unprepared to shoot is not only a tragedy for himself, his family and colleagues, but he may also put a gun in the hands of someone who is willing to turn it on innocents.

Sometimes, the only possible solution to a problem is a violent one. Soldiers who are ambushed, a police officer who is attacked while trying to make an arrest or a civilian confronted with someone determined to cause harm will have no viable alternative but to use force in self-defence. There is nothing morally superior about allowing the 'bad guys' to pound you into the pavement or even kill you. If use of armed force is the only way to win, then that is what you must do.

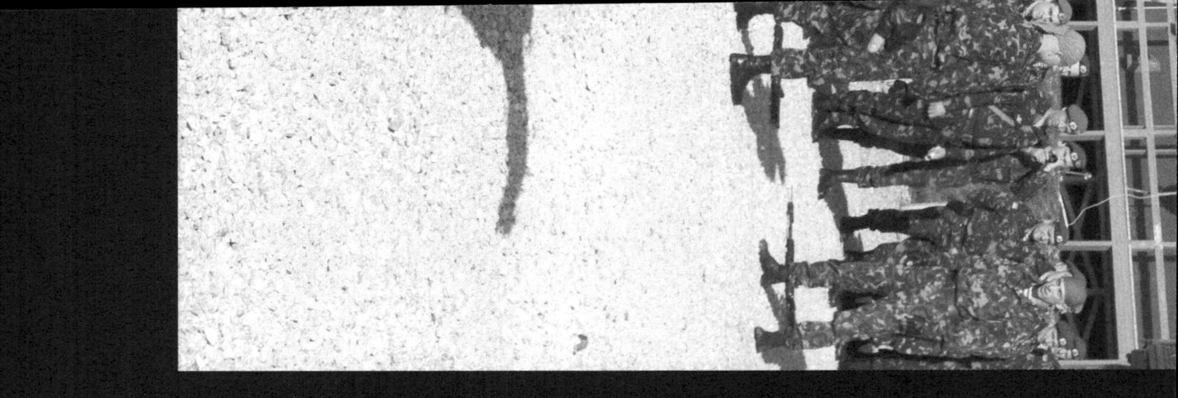

PART THREE: IN ACTION

10

Unarmed or Improvised Response

When violence starts, you fight with what you have to hand. Ideally that is the weapon you have selected and trained with, but sometimes it is whatever you can grab… or nothing at all.

There is no perfect, textbook solution to any given situation, although there are ideal outcomes. The best possibly outcome in most circumstances is a 'win' in which weapons do not have to be used; deterrence, negotiation or some other peaceful solution is generally desirable. This is not least because although violence actually does solve problems, it can often create others. Those that claim that 'violence solves nothing' are incorrect; those that say 'violence begets violence' are perhaps nearer the mark.

Some situations can be entirely resolved by violent means, but this does not mean that everything will be fine afterwards. For example, if a patrol of soldiers makes contact with a force of insurgents and wins the ensuing firefight, that problem is dealt with. However, it may be that a friend or relative of one of the dead insurgents decides to take up arms seeking revenge, where previously he would not. The initial problem has been solved; this is a new one.

Active Shooter Incident

Possibly the worst-case scenario for an unarmed person to be in is

Finding yourself unarmed in the middle of an armed incident is scary. The best course of action is to get clear and call for help, but this is not always an option.

Personal Considerations

There are also personal considerations to be taken into account. Being involved in potentially lethal combat is traumatic even if nobody is killed; those who have to take a life or seriously injure someone have to live with what they have done. This is easier to deal with if there was no real alternative, but even then there can be emotional consequences. Similarly, there may be legal questions to answer, although compliance with rules of engagement or use-of-force doctrine will protect personnel in this case.

Wherever possible, those who carry weapons would prefer to make friends, or at least make peace, than to fight. A situation that is resolved by negotiation is less likely to result in new problems than one that requires weapons use. However, when armed force is necessary it must be applied immediately and with resolve to end the matter on favourable terms. Anything less will result in defeat, and defeat in an armed fight will have serious consequences.

an active shooter incident, the situation where an individual or group enters an area and launches an attack with the intent of causing as many casualties as possible. Similar comments apply to a situation where someone runs amok with a knife, axe or similar weapon.

Attacks of this sort are often indiscriminate, although there may be a general target such as personnel at a workplace or doing a particular job. The shooter may have specific victims in mind but will injure or kill anyone in his path, possibly sparing some individuals randomly or on a whim.

An active shooter's motivations are not really relevant once the situation has begun, except perhaps to negotiators if a siege develops. What matters to anyone involved is that they are potential targets – if the shooter sees them, he may try to

Rogue Gunman

There are many reasons why someone might take a hostage, though desperation is a common one. A fleeing criminal who is cornered may take a hostage for lack of better options. This situation is more likely to be resolved by negotiation than one where hostage-taking is part of a political statement.

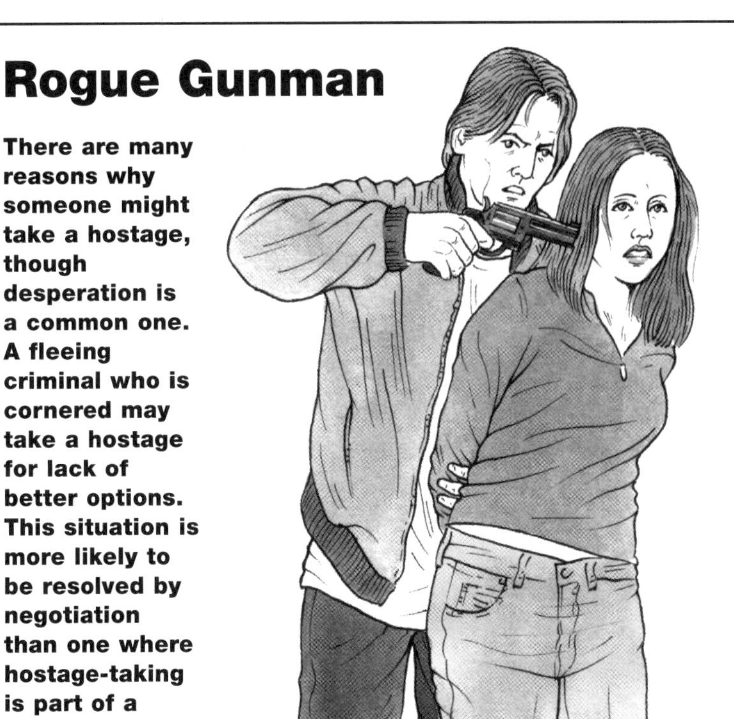

target them. Targets are normally chosen simply by availability, though the ease of making an attack may be a factor. It is possible that a shooter may concentrate on the easiest targets and ignore anyone who would be difficult to hit, but there is always the possibility that he may become focused on one particular target – even if it is someone he has never seen before – and go after them to the exclusion of easier victims.

The only sure response to an incident of this sort is to escape from the situation, evade the gunman or, if all else fails, disable him. Dissuasion and negotiation will probably not work; active shooters are often disturbed individuals whose actions are not rational, and even the threat of death may not be a deterrent. Indeed, in many cases this is a bizarre form of suicide.

Hostage Situation

A similar situation exists where hostages are taken, although the goal is not usually to immediately kill anyone. Some hostage-takers are desperate, seeking to avoid capture by the authorities. In such a case they may not have planned to take hostages and may be thinking on their feet. Others will take hostages to force compliance or hold off police response while committing a crime such as a robbery.

In both of these situations, the hostage-takers' goals are generally selfish. They want to avoid capture, escape with the money and go on living their lives as free individuals. Hostages are usually random, i.e. whoever happened to be nearby, and there will not necessarily be a deep-rooted animosity on the part of the hostage-takers. This does not mean they will not kill those who resist, or murder a hostage to reinforce their demands, but this is likely only if they become desperate.

Hostage-takers who have a political agenda often select their victims from among a group that they are opposed to, so animosity is likely to exist. In other words, politically motivated hostage-takers often view their hostages as 'the enemy' and are more likely to brutalize their captives or kill out of hand anyone they feel like. This is especially true of extremist groups. Although the hostage-situation dynamic has changed since the al-Qaeda attacks of 2001, most groups that take captives still do so as a bargaining chip rather than with the intent of killing them. They will do so, often simply to make a point, but in most situations it is possible to survive until the authorities negotiate a solution or resolve the matter by force.

However, there are situations where the hostage-takers intend from the outset to kill their captives, either for the publicity it will garner or as part of a larger scheme, such as hostages aboard an aircraft they intend to crash into a target. In such a situation, the hostages may have nothing to lose by trying to resist.

Armed Response

A hostage situation or active shooter incident will draw a response from the authorities, and possibly unofficial or semi-official attempts to stop the shooter. Responders might at first be armed citizens, security guards or lone police officers making a courageous attempt to stop the carnage as early as possible. A larger-scale response will follow, usually involving a cordon around the area and a heavily armed team moving in to deal with the aggressors. If a rescue team enters an active incident, its members will

Police Assault Team

If an assault team has to 'go in' then they will go in hard and fast. Distraction devices such as flashbangs will be used, and the team is likely to shoot anyone holding a weapon – there is rarely time for a discussion once things have reached the armed-entry point.

Special Forces Assault

Ideally, an assault makes use of surprise as well as speed and firepower. Personnel will enter the target structure by as many different routes as possible, overwhelming the defenders before an effective response can be made.

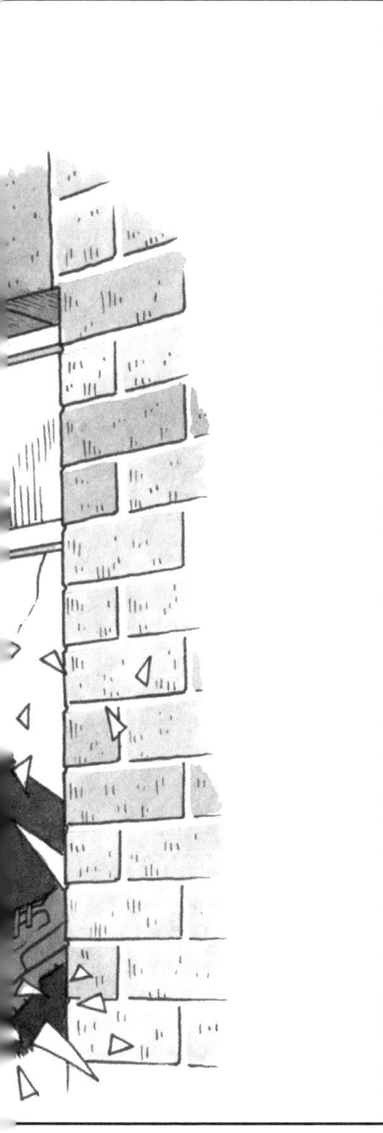

obviously attempt to preserve lives and protect the victims, but their goal must be to stop the shooting, not necessarily to assist any one individual. They will also be primed to fire on anyone with a weapon, possibly without warning. If the SWAT or Special Forces team enter a building and see an individual in civilian clothes aiming a weapon at someone, they may well shoot first and ask questions later – to do anything else would likely result in more casualties.

This does mean that mistakes can be made, but that is the price of dealing with someone intent on causing mass casualties. Innocents or responders in plain clothes need to be able to identify themselves either as the 'good guys' or as victims rather than aggressors, and one way to ensure that misidentification does not occur is to not have a visible weapon and to be acting like someone trying to escape rather than an attacker.

The first line of defence for anyone involved in an active shooting or hostage-taking situation is to escape before the aggressor(s) see them. Even those who are armed should seriously consider escape rather than attempting to deal with one or more determined opponents, especially if an official response is imminent.

Escape Route

Escape is generally a matter of getting clear of the area as quickly as possible, ideally without being spotted at all. It can be a difficult decision to make an escape if it means leaving someone behind, but sometimes there are no good options. A potential victim who escapes can raise the alarm that much earlier and may be able to provide information to the authorities about the numbers and armament of the aggressors, layout of the area and the number of victims, casualties or bystanders. They are also one less person for the responders to deal with.

Just as importantly, if someone makes the decision to escape and others will not go with them, that is their choice. Wasting time trying to convince an argumentative friend to escape may result in becoming another victim. An active shooting incident is a stark and terrible thing to be confronted with, and it requires making hard choices quickly.

Concealment

If escape from the incident is not possible, then the next best thing is concealment. A shooter will only fire at what he can see, and hostage-takers may miss some people in a building. This may create an opportunity to sneak out later, or to avoid being under the control of hostage-takers during a siege. However, any ideas about skulking around taking out the bad guys should be discarded – the key is to stay safe until the authorities bring the matter to a close. In the case of an active shooting, this will not be long, but a hostage situation may result in a protracted siege.

If it is necessary to flee from an aggressor, then contact must be broken as fast as possible. Most

Police Marksman

Police snipers generally shoot from a relatively short distance, and rarely need to be concerned with stealth or concealment – unlike their military counterparts. However, they have to operate in a cluttered urban environment, and must always be mindful of nearby innocents.

active shooters will lose interest in anyone who passes out of sight, though as already noted some will become obsessed about a single target and give chase. Hostage-takers will search for anyone they have seen, so evasion needs to be followed by escape; an active shooter may not search, so hiding is a more viable option – although escape is the ultimate goal.

The same principles apply to evading an active shooter as any other firearm attack; confusion and noise will spoil his aim, as will erratic and rapid movement.

Effective use of cover (anything that will stop a bullet) and concealment (lighter obstructions that make aiming difficult by obscuring the target) will also facilitate an escape.

Even if complete escape is not possible and attempt at evasion, or gambits like barricading doors, can be used to buy time. An active shooter may decide to go after easier targets if he encounters a locked or barricaded door, and the time taken for him to get through the door may be enough to escape by a different exit. Once he loses contact, he may break off pursuit.

Even in a worst-case scenario, where a victim is trapped with only a door between them and the gunman, the time taken to get through the door may make all the difference. The gunman may be distracted by other potential victims, taken down by law-enforcement officers, or something entirely unexpected may occur such as a collapse from the strain of his rampage. Every possible means should be used to buy time – even a few seconds could make all the difference.

It may be necessary to choose between remaining in a position of cover and making an attempt at a more complete escape. Without the means to strike back, cover and concealment offer only temporary safety. This may be enough if a response is under way – the best choice in this case is to stay behind cover and wait for the authorities to deal with the situation. If no help is immediately available, the choice is more difficult.

Breaking Cover

The risk inherent in breaking cover must be weighed against the consequences of remaining in position. Hostage-takers are likely to secure the area and then round up anyone they have not already captured, so staying under cover virtually guarantees becoming a captive. This may be a better option than being shot while fleeing, but much depends on the motives of the aggressors. An active shooter is likely to move on once he has exhausted all available targets, and will not be interested in securing the area – his aim is to kill everyone he can see, so he will go searching for more victims rather than diligently search an area already perceived as cleared.

Remaining hidden is usually a viable option with an active shooter, but there is always the possibility that he will search for victims. 'Hidden' in this case translates to 'out of sight'. People in combat or under stress will often forget about anyone who goes out of sight for a few seconds, so it may be that simply ducking behind an obstruction may be enough.

If it is not possible to escape, evade or hide from the aggressor, then fighting or surrender are the only remaining options. Surrendering to

SAS Soldier

The Special Air Service made the headlines with a high-profile assault on hostage-takers in the Iranian Embassy in London, 1980. Since then, the role of special forces in 'resolving' hostage situations has become well known and techniques are constantly refined.

hostage-takers is risky – it puts your fate entirely in their hands – but giving yourself up to an active shooter is more or less certain to be suicide. There may be a few people that any given shooter would not kill under any circumstances, but the odds are that he will simply shoot anyone who appears in his sights.

This leaves fighting as the last option. Without a weapon, the odds are not good at all. It may be possible to obtain a weapon of some kind, but this is unlikely to be a firearm. This means that the gunman must be tackled at extreme close quarters. The difficult part will be getting close enough to strike.

The best chance is an ambush, perhaps as the gunman enters a room. Distractions can also work, such as several people throwing objects at him. These don't have to be harmful; they just have to cause confusion.

Mortal Combat

If an active shooter or determined hostage-taker must be tackled, then this is an all-or-nothing situation. It is literally conquer or die. Any means whatsoever is justified (morally and legally) to defeat someone who is in the middle of a murder spree. Attacks must be made with total commitment and must be continued until the aggressor is definitely incapable of further action. Half-measures will not only result in your death, but the deaths of everyone you might have protected had you succeeded.

Law enforcement and military personnel responding to an active shooter situation or conducting an assault against hostage takers know this, and must sometimes take risks they would not consider under other circumstances. With possibly dozens of lives in the balance – including their own – they cannot afford distractions; they are there to save as many as they can by ending the situation, and that overrules the needs of any single individual.

Handgun or Knife Threat: Rear Draw

Some situations begin with the weapon already in play, but more commonly it must be deployed before it can be used. In the case of a knife or even a handgun, albeit to a lesser extent, approaching the target with weapon drawn can be counterproductive. Someone who sees a potential aggressor approaching with weapon in hand is likely to take measures to deal with the developing situation. This might include deploying a weapon of their own or fleeing.

A knife is useless against anyone who takes to his heels as the aggressor approaches, and a handgun might not be much better. Most people cannot hit a moving target with a handgun at even a modest range, so fleeing is a viable option – and most handgun users know this. Thus the weapon will probably remain concealed until the aggressor is close enough to make effective use of it.

In the case of a confrontation that escalates to the point where a weapon is produced, then obviously the weapon will need to be deployed. In this situation, just as above, the best time to deal with the weapon is as it is drawn – or ideally just before.

Concealed Carry

Many people carry their weapon in a rear position, in a holster or sheath at the back of the waistband. This is good for concealment but does require the user to put a hand behind his back in order to get at the weapon. Clothing may get in the way, slowing the draw, but whether or not it does, there are two good options: attack before the weapon is out or prevent it from being drawn.

A confrontation develops, and the defender sees the aggressor's hand disappear into the back of his waistband. That is a clear sign that it's coming back with a weapon in it. The defender acts immediately, stepping forward and delivering a strong-hand palm strike to the face. This may or may not knock the aggressor out, but the defender can take no chances – if the aggressor is sent staggering back but then pulls out his gun, he has just been given space to use the weapon more effectively.

The defender follows up his initial strike with more blows, targeting the head in the hope of knocking out the aggressor or at least disorientating him. If the aggressor brings his hands around to protect his head, then he will not be using a weapon while he does so. If he keeps trying to deploy his weapon, his head is open to attack. The defender stays close,

Bodyguard Tip: Concealment

Sometimes it is best not to reveal that you are armed. Some people use ostentatious 'minders' as a status symbol, but professional bodyguards prefer to blend in with those around them and conceal their armament. Being spotted as an armed threat can lead to becoming a priority target for the bad guys.

Blocking a Rear Draw

As the assailant reaches into the rear of his waistband for a weapon, the defender fouls the draw by sliding one arm under the weapon hand and the other over the gunman's shoulder.

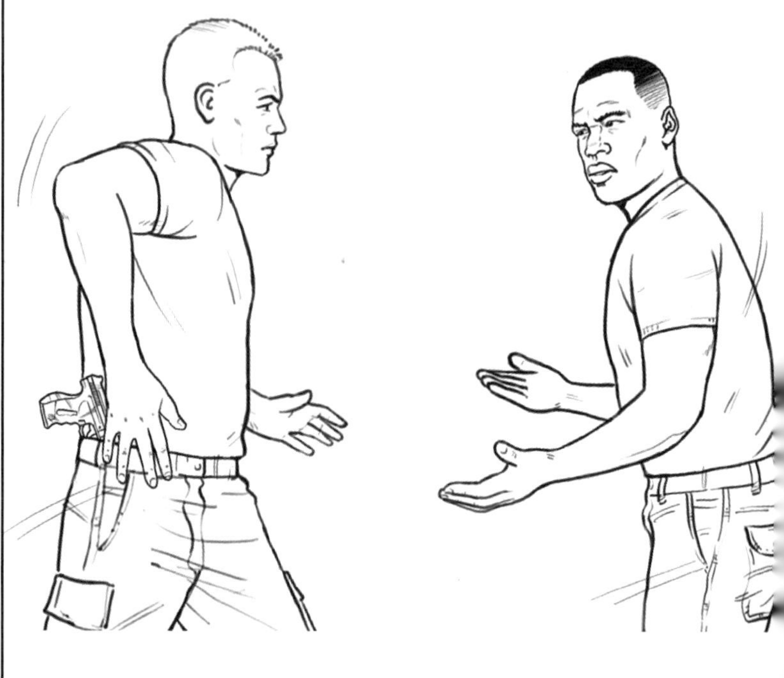

so that if the weapon does come out, it can be controlled or disarmed, but his primary intent is to render the aggressor unconscious or unable to act.

The focus here is the attacker, not the weapon. It is much easier to disarm an unconscious opponent than a conscious one, and even disarmed, a determined opponent is

With his hands locked together, the defender has immobilized the weapon. His next step is usually a takedown that causes the gunman to fall on his weapon and trap it.

still dangerous. If the guiding intellect is switched off, however, the knife or gun becomes harmless.

A weapon is useless if it cannot be deployed. The defender lunges forward while the aggressor's arm is still behind him. He shoots his own arm through and under the aggressor's weapon arm (whichever one has reached for the weapon) and reaches up his back. The defender's other arm goes over the attacker's shoulder and reaches down.

The defender brings his hands together, trapping the aggressor's weapon hand behind his back in a painful lock. The aggressor cannot slip out as his head is also in the loop of the defender's arms. The defender now takes the aggressor down so that he falls on the weapon, pinning it and his hand under him. This enables the defender to free his own hands and deliver repeated strikes to the opponent's head until he is incapacitated.

Handgun or Knife Threat: Front, Shoulder or Hip Draw

Guns are rarely carried in the front of the waistband, though some people will do so. Hip and shoulder holsters are more common, and have the advantage that the user's hand stays in front of him as he deploys his weapon. Knives may be carried in a sheath at the side of the waistband or in the front pockets of a long hoodie, which makes them easy to access without taking a hand out of the situation.

If someone reaches for a weapon carried at the front or side, he can deploy it more quickly than from a rear draw, but his wrists and forearms can be grabbed. It is still possible to launch a barrage of strikes at the weapon user's head, as above, but unless the first one puts him down, he is likely to get his weapon into play. A better option is to foul the draw.

Block the Draw

With a front or shoulder holster draw, the weapon user must put his hand across his body. If the defender lunges in and pushes the weapon hand against the body, the draw will be temporarily blocked. The weapon user may be able to back up or wriggle his weapon hand free, but while his draw is fouled the defender will be able to strike repeatedly. If the weapon user can be driven down with his weapon hand pinned, he can be taken out with blows without ever being able to clear his holster.

If the weapon does get clear of its holster, sheath or pocket, or in the case of a hip-holster draw, then the weapon arm must be controlled. It is instinctive to grab for the wrists but they are hard to get hold of and even more difficult to keep under control in a close-quarters fight. The inside of the elbow is a better target.

In this case, the defender lunges forward with one or both hands (two is better, but not always possible) and grabs the weapon arm around the elbow, pushing it back. If the weapon user's arm is pushed back behind his body, he cannot bring his weapon to bear. Once it is in this weak position, one hand can be released to deliver strikes, or the defender can then set up a disarming manoeuvre.

Blocking a Front Draw

Pushing the gunman's hand against his body will trap the weapon long enough for a strike to the throat or eyes, which can then be followed up as necessary.

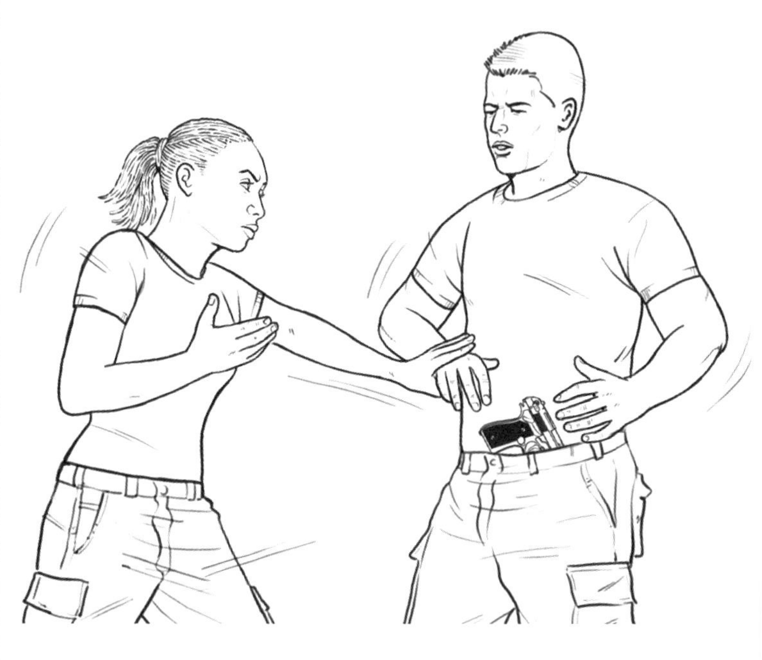

One good option from this point is to shoot the defender's outer arm through between the weapon user's arm and body, and raise it up high. The defender then turns 180 degrees so that attacker and defender are both facing the same way, and reaches down with his other hand to twist the weapon away from the aggressor. In this position, it is possible to hold him trapped with one arm up his back and beat him unconscious with his own handgun.

Knife or Handgun Threat: Front Close

Faced with either a lunging stab or an opponent who has come very close before deploying his weapon, the defender has a chance to perform an effective disarming manoeuvre that is taught in many military and police unarmed combat systems. It is known by many different names, but is sometimes simply referred to as the 'military disarm'.

Assuming a right-handed opponent, the defender deflects the weapon to his right with his right hand and while stepping left, taking himself off the line of attack. His right hand closes on the attacker's hand and wrist, grabbing whatever he can. Even a handful of sleeve is better than nothing, but a good grip can be secured using a 'stop-grip'. This means sliding down the weapon arm towards the hand as the grip is closing, until the hand stops the grab from sliding.

Military Disarm

Many military forces use some variant on this disarming move. The defender grabs the weapon arm and pivots around until he is alongside the opponent, facing the same way. He wrenches the arm up and back, using his own body as a fulcrum to break the elbow or damage the shoulder joint. The opponent is also forced down by this movement, making resistance difficult.

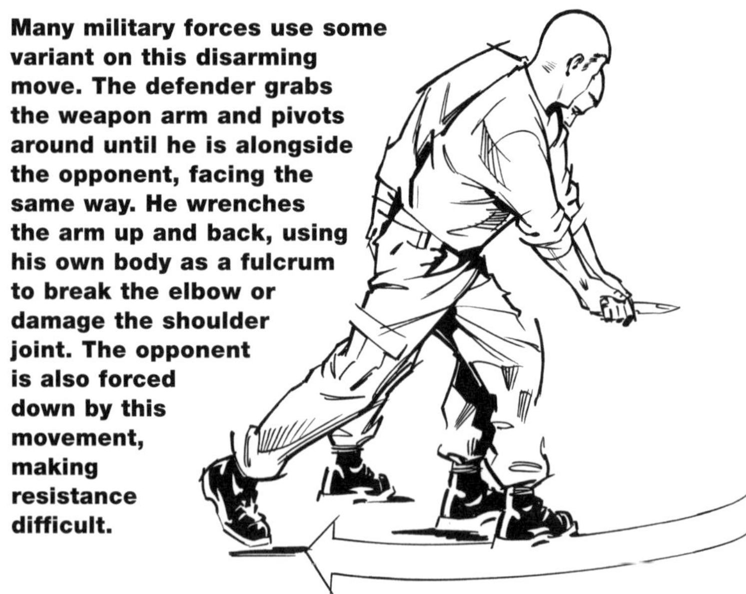

The defender now steps around 180 degrees, pulling the weapon arm around with him as he drops an elbow strike into the back of the arm to break it. Even if this does not work, he uses his elbow as a fulcrum as he yanks the weapon arm up and back, pushing down on the back of the weapon user's shoulder and arm to force him down. The defender's hand slides onto the weapon and twists it away as he tries to slam the weapon user face-first into the ground. The combination of twisting the weapon against the hand and wrist, and applying pressure on the arm and shoulder, should deprive the aggressor of his weapon.

Although this movement is intended as a disarm, if it succeeds in breaking the weapon user's arm then that can be considered a good enough result for military purposes. The aim is to stop him using his weapon, not necessarily to perform

Knife Disarms

I get asked 'do you teach knife disarms?' from time to time. My answer is no, I don't. I will, however, teach you to deal with someone armed with a knife. That may or may not include disarming him, but the key is to deal with the situation (an attacker armed with a knife) and not to fixate on getting the weapon away from him. If he takes it back and stabs you, or beats you senseless while you have the knife, you have not won.

A knife disarm is something you might do to deal with an armed threat, but it is necessary to have a range of responses in mind in case simply disarming the opponent is not the best option.

a neat and tidy disarming technique. The same movement can be used, less violently, to control a suspect.

Handgun or Knife Threat: One-Handed Grip

There are two good options against a one-handed handgun or knife threat. One is to simply push the weapon aside and strike the aggressor. Obviously, a strike that does not immediately disable the weapon user must be followed up, and the weapon may come back into play if it is not controlled. This is therefore a somewhat risky strategy, but it can be an effective opening that then allows the weapon to be controlled.

A palm strike to the jaw may knock the weapon user out, or a strike to the throat may incapacitate or even kill him. A 'web hand' or 'cradle' strike is best for this purpose. This strike uses the web of the hand between thumb and first finger to strike the throat as hard as possible. A stiff-fingered jab into the throat is also effective, and an eye strike with slightly spread fingers may work. The latter will cause the opponent to flinch but will not normally end the situation unless it is vigorously followed up.

In this case, the defender clears the weapon from the line of attack for long enough to disable the opponent,

One-handed Grip 1

Against a one-handed grip, it is possible to grab the weapon by the barrel and twist it up and outward, to point away from your head. Move suddenly and follow up with strikes to the head or throat with the free hand.

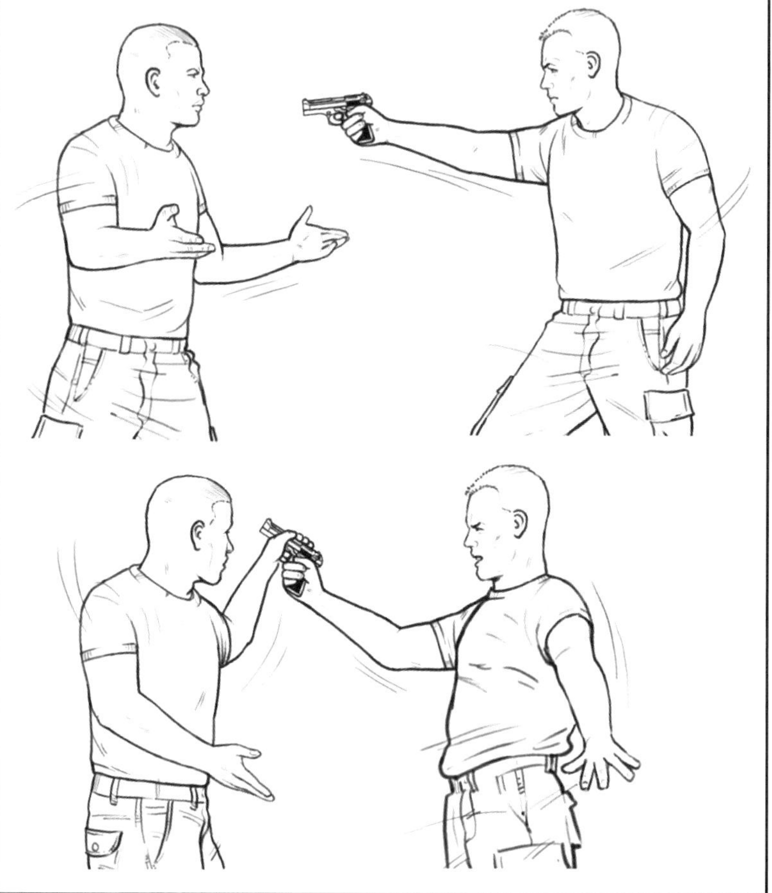

One-handed Grip 2

If your nearest hand is on the outside or is high enough, you can instead twist the weapon inward. In this case, the best follow-up is to pull the weapon grip-first towards you. If the opponent lets go, you have his weapon. If not, he will be pulled onto a strike to the face or throat.

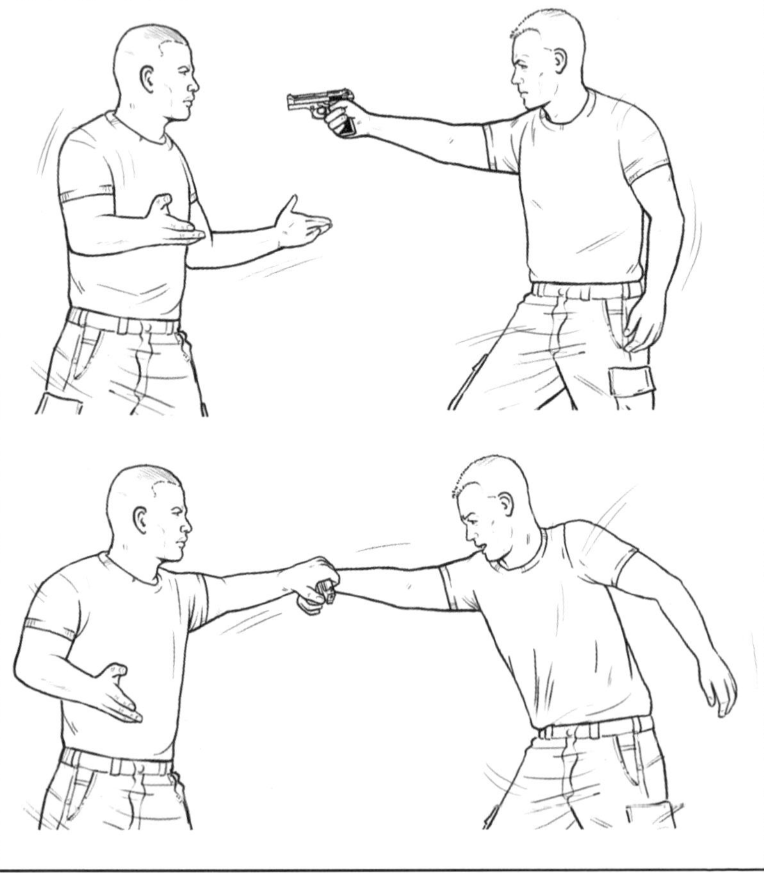

and does not attempt to control it as such. Of course, a weapon in the hand of someone who is choking or unconscious is, to all intents and purposes, controlled, but this remains a risky option.

As an alternative, the defender can attempt to disarm the opponent. If his hand is below the weapon, he moves forward and to his right, off the line of attack, and at the same time pushes the weapon sharply up and to his left with the web of his left hand. His fingers close around the top of the weapon and he twists the barrel up sharply before pulling it down and towards his own hip. His aim is to twist the weapon so far that the muzzle is pointing away from him, back over the user's shoulder, and then to yank it out of his hand.

The weapon can also be twisted outwards, but this is a weaker action and may allow the user to retain his hold. Striking him in the face or throat with the free hand can facilitate a disarm.

If the defender's hand is higher than the weapon, he might instead step to his left, bringing his hand sharply around (thumb towards himself) to grasp the top of the weapon, which can then be pulled or twisted out of the user's hand. If a handgun is pulled forward, it will discharge, so it is vital to ensure that it is pointed past the defender. In some circumstances it is possible to present the handgrip of the weapon to the defender's strong hand, enabling him to use the weapon almost instantly.

Handgun Threat, Front: Two-Handed Grip

A two-handed shooting stance creates a strong lock on the weapon, and requires both hands to break. One option is to move slightly off the line of fire and push the weapon up and back with the web of the left hand, grasping it around the top with the fingers and twisting upwards as if trying to point the muzzle at the user's face. At the same time, the defender steps round to the right and smashes his forearm down on the inside of one or both of the weapon user's arms. This should fold the elbow.

The result of this movement is that the weapon user finds his handgun turning over to point at his face, making him very unlikely to pull the trigger. The handgun can then be pulled forward and down to disarm the user. The weapon may discharge at this point, and if it does, the user may shoot himself in the face. Disarming him becomes a lot easier at that point.

As an alternative to this movement, the defender drives his right arm vertically down between the weapon user's forearms, then uses this arm as a pry bar to rotate the user's grip off his weapon. He ends up with the

Two-handed Handgun Disarm

A two-handed stance is harder to disarm. The defender moves to the side and pushes the weapon up and away from him with his lead hand, then pivots in to face the same way as the opponent (B). He forces his other hand down between the opponent's arms (C) and then pivots back to his original position, ensuring that the weapon points past him the whole time.

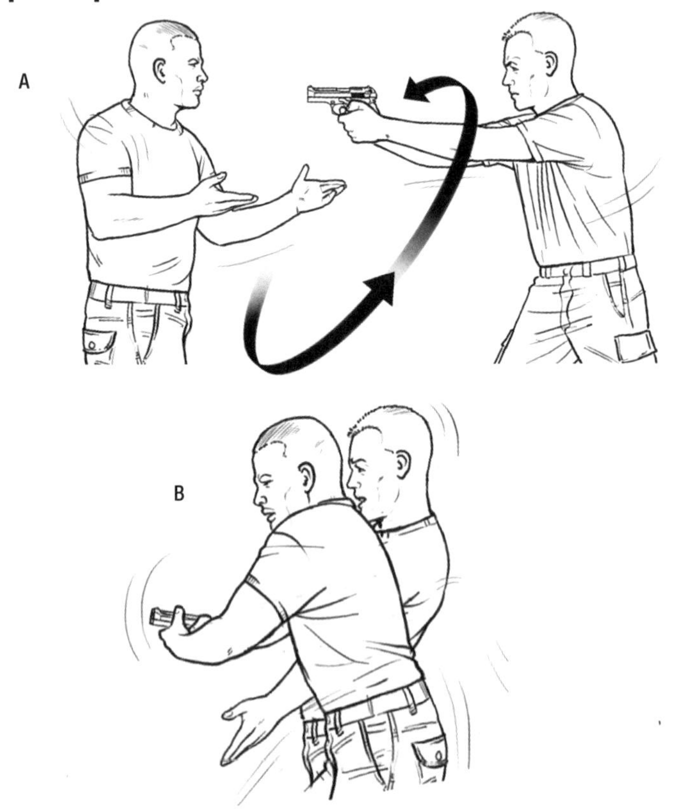

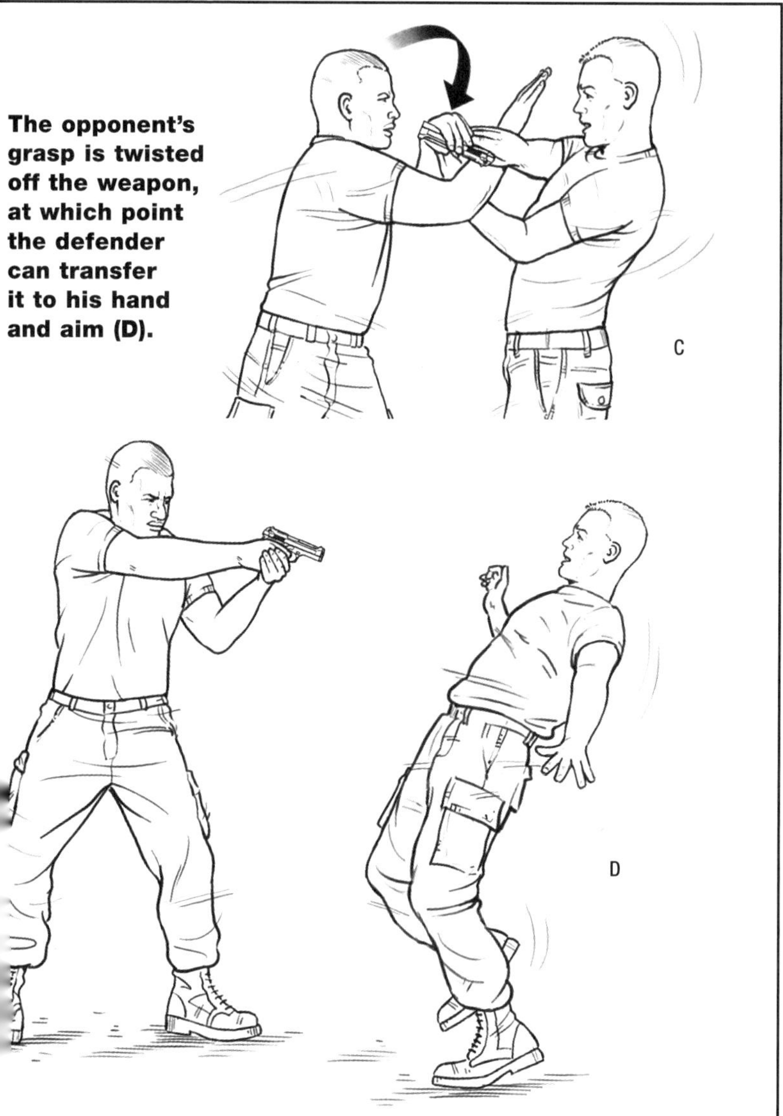

The opponent's grasp is twisted off the weapon, at which point the defender can transfer it to his hand and aim (D).

Handgun Disarm

An alternative disarm for a two-handed stance begins with the defender pushing the weapon up and back with his nearest hand. He then closes in and slams his forearm down on the crook of the opponent's arms. This folds the arms and allows the weapon to point up at the owner's face.

Low Rear Handgun Threat

The soldier turns and sweeps the weapon away, but cannot immediately control the weapon arm as his arm is not well positioned (B). Instead, he drives his elbow into the gunman (C), keeping the weapon pointed away from him by pulling it with his other hand until he can get the weapon arm under control.

High Rear Handgun Threat

The soldier turns suddenly, knocking the weapon aside and controlling it by wrapping the weapon arm with his own. The muzzle is past him and thus not an immediate threat (B).

He follows up with an elbow strike to the face, tipping the opponent's head back and unbalancing him, and hooks away his foot (C). Still keeping the weapon immobilized, he uses a knee-drop onto the opponent's body and delivers strikes to the head (D).

weapon held by the barrel in his left hand, presenting the grip to his strong hand.

Rear Weapon Threat

Threatened with a gun or knife from behind, the defender needs to know where the weapon is. This is usually obvious, but a quick, 'nervous' glance while seeming to comply with demands will confirm its location. The defender may raise his hands as if surrendering – this is a fairly natural response and should not arouse suspicion.

Ideally, the defender turns and sweeps the weapon aside. The height at which he sweeps with his arm is of course determined by the height of the weapon. If the defender turns 'inside' the weapon it may be possible to wrap an arm around the user's weapon arm and immobilize him, delivering heavy blows to the head and throat. If the defender has turned 'outside' the weapon, then a movement similar to the military disarm described above can be used.

Longarm Threat

A longarm such as a rifle or shotgun can be dealt with in a similar manner to disarming a handgun. However, the extra length of the weapon can make it difficult to get control of the trigger hand. One option is snaking an arm around the barrel, which will immobilize the weapon and also trap the user's arms, rendering him vulnerable to a barrage of strikes. As with handgun threats, it is vital to push the weapon aside; once it is pointing away from the defender, it is less of a threat.

Bayonet Defence

The mounted bayonet has a long reach and is often lethal, but in many ways bayonet defence is similar to dealing with a frontal longarm threat. The defender evades the strike by moving to the side and pushing the weapon away, and closes in to get 'past the point'. This also protects him from an attempt to shoot with the rifle. So long as the rifle is controlled and cannot come to bear, it is no longer much of a threat to the defender.

From this position, the defender can attack the weapon user's arm, trying to break it. Even if this fails, it may still dislodge his grip from the rifle or bend him over where he is vulnerable to being kicked. The rifle can also be twisted forward and away from the user, or the defender may be able to get around behind him and apply a chokehold.

Alternatively, repeated elbow strikes to the side of the head can be delivered from very close range and will eventually convince the user to let go of his rifle, or simply make him incapable of retaining it by rendering him unconscious.

Bayonet Stab Defence

With any stabbing attack, the weapon will move directly towards the target. By stepping to the side and deflecting the weapon, the soldier creates an opportunity to counterattack (A). He seizes the opponent's arm and attempts an arm break (B), using pressure on the arm to push his opponent's head down (C). A kick to the face should take him out of the fight (D).

Longarm Disarm

The defender deflects a bayonet thrust or the muzzle and moves in, snaking his arm around the weapon to immobilize it. He then delivers punishing strikes to the groin and head or throat.

Secure That Weapon

IIt takes little effort to lift and fire a handgun, and even a severely wounded opponent can still kill someone. All military and law enforcement personnel are taught to secure any weapon that is dropped, and at the very least to move weapons away from disabled opponents. Even if an aggressor is down and presumed dead, trained people will not leave a weapon lying close to his hand. The moment it takes to kick a weapon aside is time well spent.

Fighting For a Gun or Knife

Few defences ever go as well as planned, and often it is necessary to fight for the weapon. A simple rule is 'both hands on the wheel', i.e. both hands are used to control the weapon or weapon hand. Even if the weapon user is punching with the other hand, the weapon is the greater threat and must be kept from being used. Once the weapon is in a position where it can be kept under control with one hand, it is possible to free the other to fight with.

When fighting for a weapon, there are two options – disable the user or get his weapon away from him. The latter is often followed by disablement anyway, especially in a military context, but it is easier to defeat a disarmed opponent. Disablement usually means striking the groin, head or throat until the weapon user cannot fight any more.

Disarming an opponent is normally done either by taking the weapon from his limp fingers after disabling him or by twisting the weapon against his hand. The key here is to keep a sharp object immobile and a firearm pointed anywhere but at the defender. If the weapon can be twisted against the user's range of hand or wrist motion, it will come out of his hand. Note that it is perfectly possible to push on the side of a knife blade – it only cuts in the direction of the edge.

Once the weapon is freed from the user's grasp, he does not instantly become harmless. He can still fight, and may be able to get his weapon back. Thus it is vital not to fixate on the weapon – the opponent is dangerous, and more so with a weapon in hand, while the weapon itself is merely a tool.

Dealing With a Heavy Blunt Weapon

If an opponent picks up a heavy blunt weapon, trying to disarm him is usually a bad idea. His primary attack is an overhead strike, and an attempt to disarm will usually result in the weapon falling on one or both of the combatants. This can be something of a lottery and is best avoided. Likewise, coming in with a kick or similar attack can result in

Defending an Overhead Swing

The soldier steps out from under the weapon's arc rather than trying to block it directly (A).

the heavy weapon falling on the defender. A far better option is to let the opponent tire himself trying to use an unsuitable heavy implement and to evade it if he attempts to strike. Stepping out to either side will cause the weapon to miss and enables the defender to close in for a strike of his own while the weapon user is over-committed. This strike might be made with a weapon or an unarmed blow may suffice.

He pushes the opponent's arms down as the strike goes past, making it harder to recover from the missed strike (B). While the opponent is still off balance, the soldier then delivers a low roundhouse kick to the back of the legs (C).

11

With Blunt Weapons

Blunt weapons can be used both defensively and offensively, and do not require great skill to be effective.

Blunt implements are easy to improvise even if a purpose-made weapon is not available. They usually have the mass and solid construction required to block an attack and are instinctive to use. This can be important under the stress of close combat, as a blunt weapon does not require great precision and even a marginal hit will get some kind of result.

Front Threat

Faced with a hostile who has started to reach for a weapon, or who has deployed one but not yet begun an action that requires a defensive response, the defender takes the initiative by launching a strike of his own. Sometimes attacking can be an effective defence, either by forcing the opponent onto the defensive or taking him out before he can make his own attack. Most people expect a blunt weapon to be swung, so the defender gains the advantage of surprise by jabbing the opponent in the body with a bayonet-style strike. This will not end a fight but it will cause shock and pain, and will often pull the opponent's head forward where it can be easily struck. Keeping both hands on the weapon, the

While few people carry a stick around with them, stick-fighting skills carry over to many other, similar objects.

Push Strike and Follow-up

A two-handed push strike can be followed up by letting go of one end of the stick and delivering a rapid strike to the head, using primarily wrist action.

Stick Jab to Face

As the attacker chambers for a backhand strike, the soldier lunges in and delivers a jabbing strike to the face. This will disrupt the attacker's intentions and serves as an alternative to blocking the strike.

defender now jabs upward under the chin. This was taught to World War II commandos as a killing stroke, and like all attacks to the throat it should be used only where necessary.

As an alternative to jabbing, the defender can make a pushing strike to the opponent's face with the weapon held horizontally in both hands. This has the advantage of surprising most aggressors, who might expect a more conventional attack, and also halting any movement forward on their part. Immediately after striking the opponent, the defender releases one end of the weapon and whips it around with the other hand, striking the side of the head.

A similar movement can be used to block an overhead blow, launching the strike as the opponent's weapon rebounds from the block. The main difference is that instead of pushing the weapon out forwards, the defender must direct its energy upwards to intercept the attack, and raise it high enough to protect his head.

Forehand Strike

If the opponent has already begun an attack then this must be dealt with before any counterattack can be made. It might be possible to evade the attack and strike without blocking, but often a block is necessary to completely halt the opponent's strike.

Faced with a forehand strike, the defender performs a roof block, closing in as he does so. He rests his own weapon against his arm for additional strength, taking care to keep his arm inside the protection of it. As the opponent's attack is deflected, the defender grabs his weapon arm and pulls him off balance, striking with a forehand blow of his own. If the opponent is very close, a hammer strike with the base of the weapon might be more effective.

Backhand Strike

Faced with a backhand strike, the defender makes a stick-up block and steps in close, raising his weapon to drop a hammer strike onto the opponent's head or shoulder. His arm remains between the opponent's weapon and his body in case of a renewed attack, which would not generate much force in the distance available. If the opponent scrambles backwards, the defender can turn his hammer strike into a downward forehand blow with his weapon, following the same path.

Knife Slash

As the opponent makes a slash, the defender sidesteps away from the knife and turns so that he is still facing the opponent. He brings his weapon down sharply onto the opponent's forearm. This may break the arm or jerk it so that the weapon is dropped; certainly it will weaken the opponent's weapon arm. Attempting to strike

High Block and Counterattack

The soldier defends against a forehand strike by making a stick-down block with the weapon additionally supported on his shoulder. He reaches in at the same time with his weak-side hand and 'snakes' it around the opponent's arm, immobilising it. He then delivers a downward hammer strike with the end of his stick.

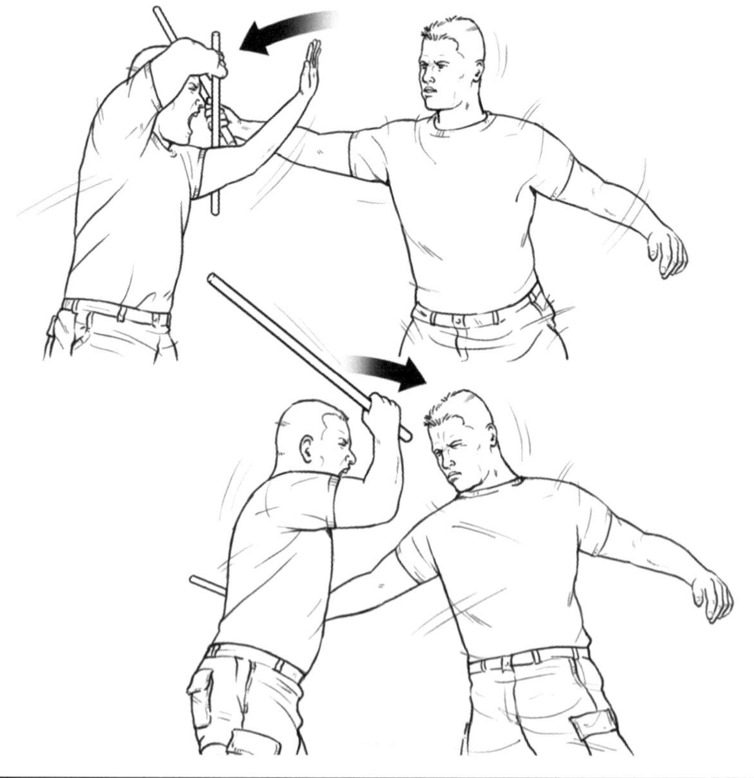

Stick Up Block and Counterattack

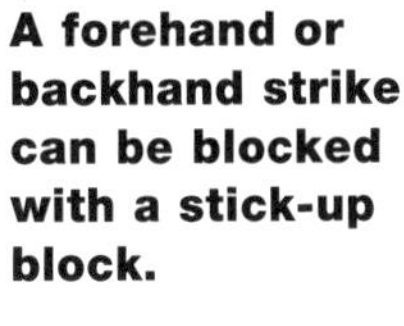

A forehand or backhand strike can be blocked with a stick-up block.

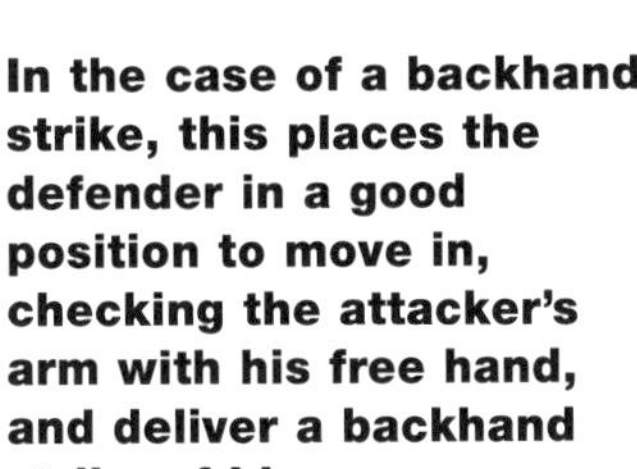

In the case of a backhand strike, this places the defender in a good position to move in, checking the attacker's arm with his free hand, and deliver a backhand strike of his own.

Sidestep and Counterstrike

Faced with a knife thrust, the defender moves sideways and deflects the strike with his free hand, attacking the opponent's leg at the same time. Against a slash he does much the same but as his free hand checks the slash, his stick strikes the weapon arm to disable it.

the knife would require too much precision to be a viable option under most circumstances – the arm is a better target.

The arm strike is followed through downwards, and is immediately countered with a backhand blow to the opponent's leg or knee. The defender is now placed to the side of the opponent and well positioned to deliver more strikes until the threat is nullified.

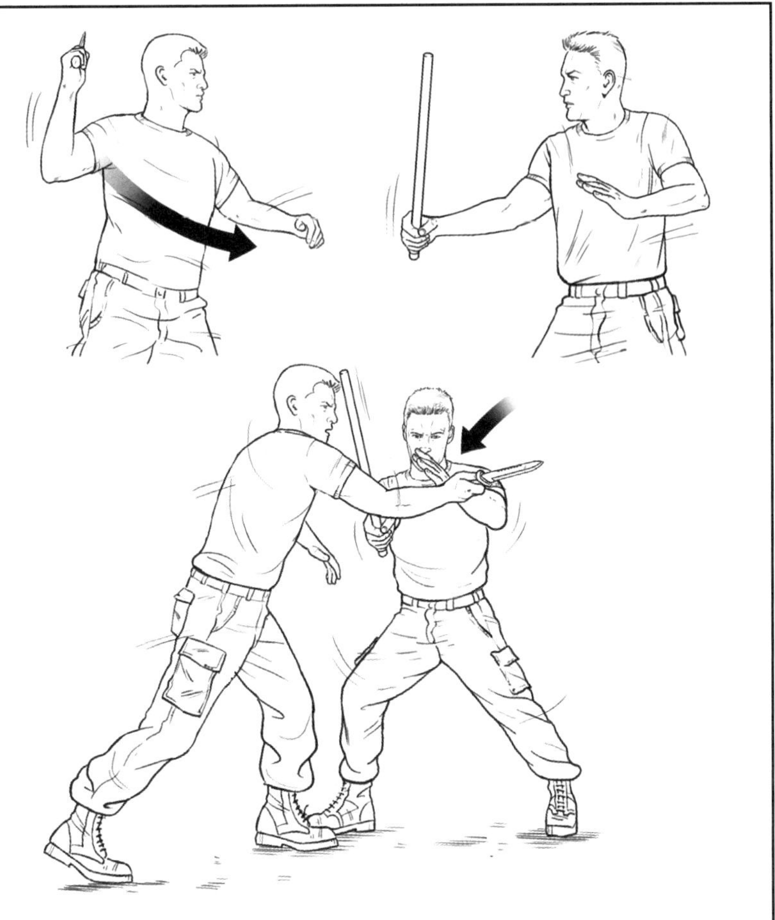

Knife Stab

Faced with a frontal knife stab, the defender sweeps his weapon in a semicircular motion that is partially a deflection and partially a strike to the weapon arm. As noted above he does not attempt to hit the knife, as disabling the arm that controls it is a better option. The defender follows up with a forehand strike to the head. He circles away from the direction his blow sent the knife and moves back a little in order to make use of his weapon's greater reach. If he can prevent the knife user from getting close enough to stab, and strikes him every time he tries, he can end the fight with minimal risk to himself.

Kubotan Grab Release

Equipped only with a short stick or similar item such as a metal pen, the defender needs to dislodge an opponent's grip. Holding his weapon in an icepick grip or in the middle so that part of it sticks out, he delivers a sharp blow to the opponent's collarbone, neck, temple or the side of his head. This will cause most opponents to flinch and let go of their own accord. The initial forehand hammer strike is followed up by a backhand strike to the face, and the defender's free hand can peel the attacker's grip off at the same time this strike is launched. A cycle of forehand-backhand-forehand blows can then be delivered, or repeated hammer strikes can be dropped into the opponent's forehead and face.

There are more subtle ways to use a Kubotan, but this quick-and-dirty method will secure a fast release. Alternative targets include the opponent's grabbing arm. His hand can also be struck, but this does risk the defender hitting himself instead. If there is no room to strike, the Kubotan can be held in a knife-style grip and ground into the opponent's neck or throat, or up under his chin. A thumb in the same place will also serve as well, but a hard object works much better.

Multiple Attackers

Faced with multiple attackers, the defender does not have time to pick and choose where he strikes, and cannot afford to become surrounded or grabbed and pinned. He must keep moving, ideally causing the attackers to get in each other's way, and must strike at whatever targets present themselves.

The defender can of course attack whenever the opportunity arises, but must avoid becoming over-committed. A barrage of strikes that takes one opponent out of the fight is of little use if someone else moves around behind the defender and hits him over the head. Thus a policy of hit-and-run is wise, even if it means passing up a chance to put one of the opponents down. The key is to remain capable of fighting and take chances to strike back as they come.

The defender might fake an attack at one opponent to make him retreat a couple of steps, gaining time to strike another opponent. He might strike an opponent's leg, slowing him, and move so that the disabled opponent is left behind. If an opportunity arises to put one of the hostiles out of the fight, he will take it, but any blow that weakens an opponent is a step towards eventual victory.

Controlling the Weapon Arm

If the attacker does not quickly retract his weapon arm after making a strike, the defender can grab it and gain control of his weapon. He will then have no defence against a return blow.

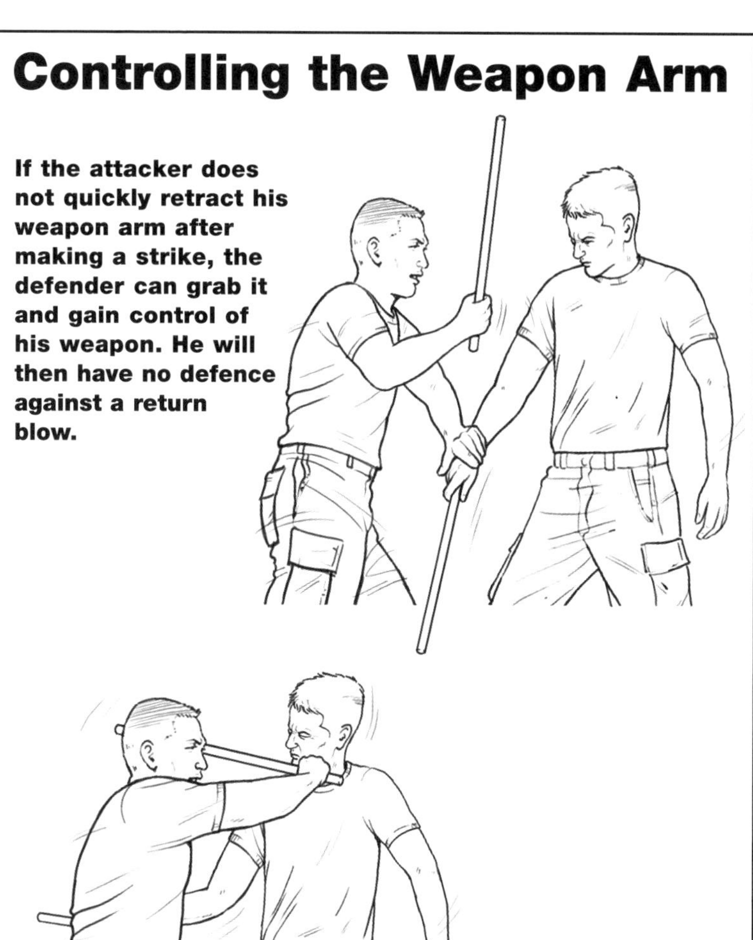

12

Sharp and pointed weapons can cause serious injury even with a marginal hit.

With Sharp or Pointed Weapons

Sharp and pointed weapons can be considered to be killing rather than fighting tools. The injuries they cause tend to be severe, even on a marginal hit, and usually require medical assistance. Thus it is relatively easy to give an opponent a wound that will cause him to want to break off the action and get help, at least if he is in a rational state of mind. However, it is also easy to kill when the intent was simply to wound. Most sharp or pointed weapons are not well suited to blocking strikes, as they lack mass in most cases. There are exceptions, such as swords and machetes, but for the most part defence is performed with the unarmed hand or by evasion.

Knife Attack

If necessary, the defender can mitigate the damage by covering the ribs or neck and head with the arm. A cut to the outside of the arm is serious, but serious is better than fatal – and a cut to the neck is likely to result in death. A serious cut on the arm may be a fair price for winning a knife fight. However, ideally the defender completely protects himself – at least for long enough to win the fight.

Skill is needed to inflict damage with a sharp or pointed weapon if the opponent is fighting back with a weapon of his own.

The defender deflects the slash by circling away from it and slapping or pushing the attacker's arm. At the same time he makes a forehand cut of his own. This can be directed at the neck, to kill, or against the weapon arm. If the defender is quick, he can pull his cut towards himself then reverse the direction of his knife, stabbing the opponent in the chest with a short movement.

If the defender is holding his knife in an icepick grip, he can use his weapon to back up his defensive arm movement. The attacker's slash brings his arm into contact with the defender's blade. As soon as the contact is felt, the

Hunting Knife and Bayonet

The length of blade on a knife dictates how far it will penetrate on a thrust, and to some extent how well it will cut. A penetrating wound need only be 5cm deep to cause a potentially life-threatening injury.

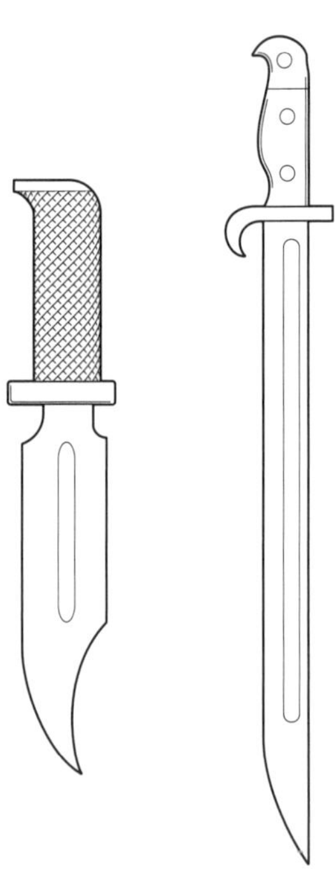

Offhand Parry and Counterattack

Most commonly, the knife is used for any counterattack that is to be made. However, there are times when an immediate cut or stab might not be the most effective response. A blow to the head has opened the opponent's neck up for a killing slash.

Icepick Grip

The 'icepick grip' or 'reverse grip' is well suited to short, hard, stabbing motions and short slashes. It requires some skill to make best use of this position.

defender drags his knife across the opponent's arm, hoping to disable it. He can then follow up with a slash across the attacker's face or throat, and a hammer strike-style stab downwards into the upper chest.

Knife Stab

The defender deflects the stab to one side with his unarmed hand, ideally also moving out of its path. At the same time he slashes at the attacker. It is sometimes possible to end a knife fight without someone dying by cutting across the brow. This causes a messy wound that bleeds enormously (like most head wounds). Blood in the eyes will blind the attacker, and the graphic nature of the injury may even discourage his comrades.

More commonly, the defender will simply slash whatever he can reach. This may be the attacker's arm, face or throat, and may or may not kill him. Precision is difficult when under attack with a sharp implement, so most knife fighters will follow up their cut with others until they succeed in doing enough damage to stop the opponent.

Stick Attack

Faced with a stick or similar implement, the defender armed with a knife has a reach disadvantage but may be able to deter attack by virtue of his weapon's superior lethality. If this does not work then he must get inside the reach of the opponent's weapon, closing in to where he has the advantage.

As the opponent makes a forehand swing, the defender moves inside the arc of the weapon, covering his head with his free arm. He needs to get close enough that the attacker's arm, not the stick, hits his guarding arm. The block can be augmented using the knife, by turning into the arc and using both arms to defend. This allows a quick cut across the attacker's weapon arm, which may disable it.

As the stick hits his covering arm, the defender 'snakes' his arm over and around the opponent's weapon arm, immobilizing it. He can now

Icepick Grip: Good or Bad?

The icepick grip is useful for defensive movements with a knife, but is limited offensively. A huge overhead stab, favoured by people taking part in martial arts demonstrations, leaves the attacker wide open to whatever the defender feels like doing to him. Thus as a rule there are two kinds of people who use the icepick grip – those who are well trained and have made a tactical choice to maximize the defensive advantages it gives, and those who have absolutely no idea what they are doing.

Knife Fight

The defender has protected his torso and neck with the outside of his arm (A), ensuring that any cut taken there will not hit an artery.

He counters with a slash to the arm (B) and immediately follows up with a thrust to the body (C), all the time keeping control of the opponent's knife arm.

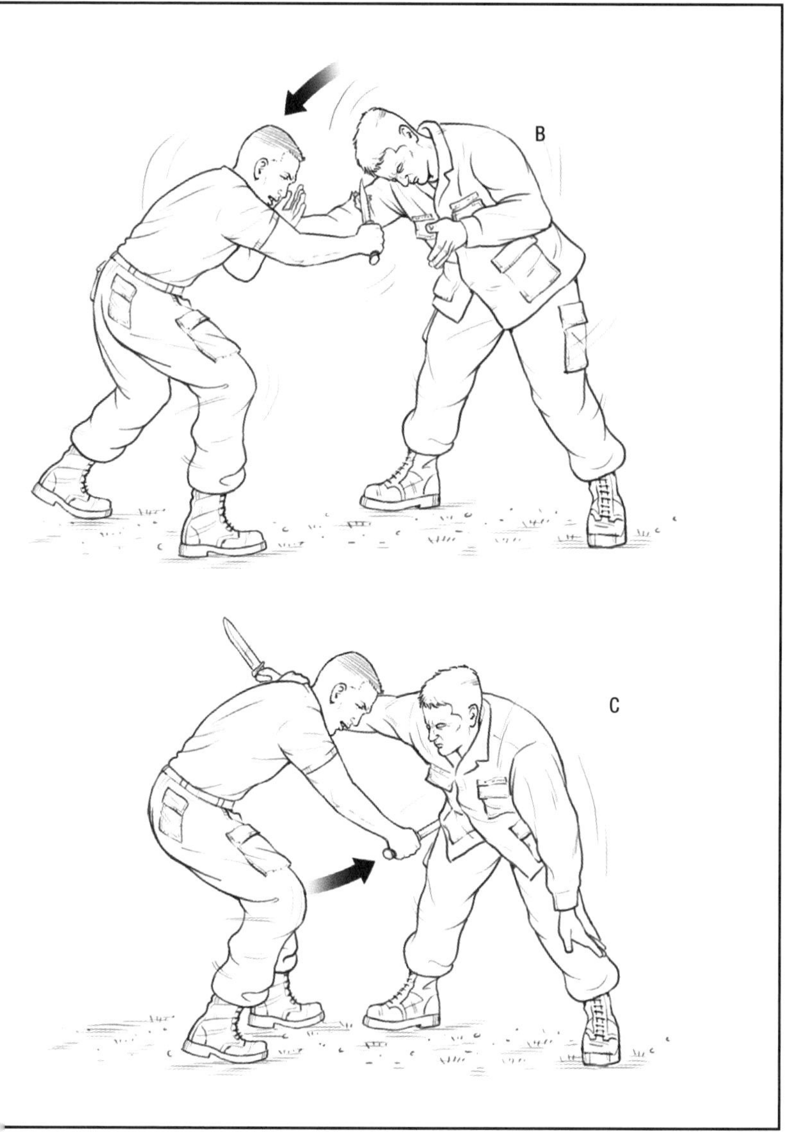
B
C

Knife vs Blunt Weapon

1. The defender protects his head using his arm, moving in so that the attacker's arm and not the stick strikes his defence.

2. The defender makes an immediate knife thrust to the body before his opponent can recover from his failed strike.

pull the opponent on to a knife stab, or disarm him using the weapon as a threat. This can be done in one of two ways.

Option one is to put the knifepoint to the opponent's chest or throat and demand that he drops the weapon. The main problem with this is that it takes time to give the command and for the opponent to comply. In the middle of a struggle the opponent may not hear or comprehend what has been said, and might use the delay in waiting for him to relinquish his weapon to free it or grab the knife hand.

Option two is to strip the stick out of the opponent's hand by stepping back and pulling up and back with the unarmed hand, which remains wrapped around the opponent's weapon arm. This movement can be thwarted by moving forward, so the defender uses the threat of his knife to push the opponent back. The combination of attacker moving his head and body back, away from the knife, and defender pulling

3. Alternatively, the defender can snake his arm around the stick to control it...

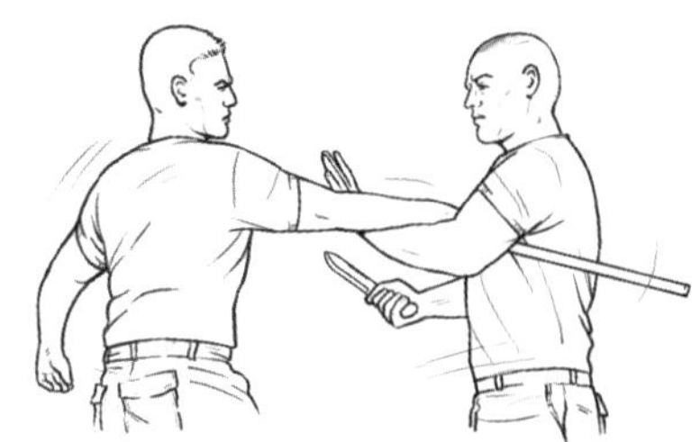

4. ...and by pulling his arm backwards can 'strip' the stick out of the attacker's hand. At the same time, he thrusts out the knife as a threat.

the weapon up and away from its user, will cause it to come free and either fall to the ground or, ideally, be grabbed by the defender ready for use.

Disarming an Opponent

Disarming an opponent is not always an option in the chaos of combat. If the defender needs to, he can defend against a forehand strike by circling away from it and palming the opponent's weapon arm away while slashing at his head or arm with the knife. A cut across the neck will bring the matter to a quick, if messy, finish.

Facing a backhand blow, the defender can jam the strike by pushing the attacker's arm towards his head or chest with the unarmed hand. The defender can then close in and stab underneath the attacker's arm. He will not be able to see the stab coming as his own arm blocks his view. As a less fatal option, the defender might choose to slash the attacker's weapon arm or the hand holding the weapon.

13

Guns can do the greatest damage most easily, but require some ability to use effectively.

Fighting with Guns

Personnel equipped with firearms have different options to those with hand weapons, but are not necessarily invulnerable. A gun user needs to keep his opponent at a reasonable distance – shooting someone who is rushing forward with a hand weapon may not stop them in time to prevent them from making a fatal attack.

At extreme close quarters, it is still possible to shoot if the weapon can be brought to bear, but even an unarmed opponent can defeat a gun user if he can grab the weapon or the arm that holds it. Indeed, several police officers have been killed because assailants were able to grab their weapon arm and they were unable to free it in time.

Some people who carry weapons in their daily lives train their loved ones to walk on their unarmed side, or brief them on what to do if a confrontation develops. This generally comes down to getting out of the line of fire, seeking cover and above all not grabbing at their partner as he or she attempts to deploy a weapon. Police officers and some military personnel are also trained in weapon retention techniques, which generally take the form of freeing the

Short-range gunfights tends to be over fairly quickly. Normally, one side is quickly defeated or seeks cover and then disengages.

Law Enforcement Tip: Always...

Always assume that any weapon is loaded and in a condition to fire unless you know it is not. Do not make assumptions. Check.

arm from a grab and pushing away whoever has hold of it.

Shooting from the Draw

When shooting with a handgun, ideally both hands need to be on the weapon to control it properly. A good, firm stance not only acts as a platform for accurate shooting but can also deter a potential assailant – the stance suggests that the gun user knows his business and is both willing to fire and able to hit the target.

When drawing a handgun, the weak-side foot moves forward and the shooter lowers his centre of gravity for stability. The weak hand clears clothing aside if necessary, then moves forward as the strong hand grips the weapon. The strong hand comes to meet the weak one as the weapon comes into line with the user's eyes. A solid lock is established as the weak hand pulls back towards the user and the strong hand pushes forward. Many shooters are trained to push the muzzle of the weapon at the target as if trying to stab it. From this

Draw and Shoot

position, the gun user can shoot immediately or use his weapon as a deterrent. If he must move or shift position, he moves as smoothly as possible, knees bent to disturb the aim point as little as possible.

If the threat is extremely close, a one-handed shooting position might be used instead. In this case the lead hand is pushed out to check the opponent's forward movement, and the weapon is brought up to just above hip height, well back and out of reach of the opponent. This prevents the weapon from being grabbed and may stop an advancing opponent from landing a strike with fists or a hand weapon.

The handgun user first clears clothing out of the way, then draws his weapon. He pushes it out at the target as if trying to stab it with the muzzle, establishing a two-handed grip on the weapon as he does so.

Foiling a Handgun Grab

Someone who is reaching for a handgun can be sharply pushed away using the free hand (A).

If a grab has already been established, the key is to break the grip. This usually requires sharply twisting the weapon arm while pushing the opponent away (B).

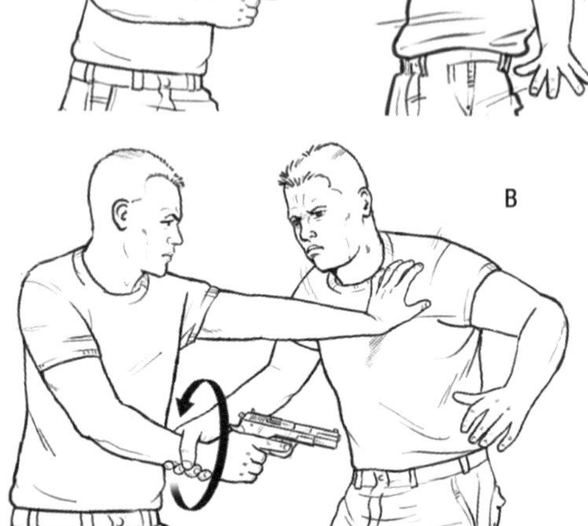

If the grip cannot be instantly broken, alternative options include striking the opponent with the free hand (C). Movements need to be short and violent, ideally causing the opponent to lose his balance.

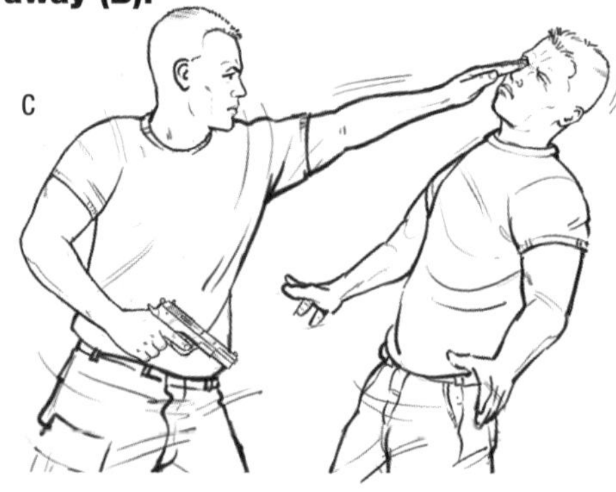

Special Forces Tip: Hold It Properly!

Holding a handgun sideways 'gangsta fashion' suggests that you consider the weapon to be a fashion accessory rather than a tool. Hold your weapon properly so that you can control and retain it. Apart from anything else, waving a weapon around in an undisciplined fashion is alarming to people on your side that actually know what they are doing. It certainly does not inspire confidence in your ability to deal with a situation.

A similar position is often used when moving through a building. The lead hand can check anyone who suddenly appears and lunges at the gun user, and there is no danger of the weapon being knocked out of the user's hand as he passes someone concealed in a doorway or around a corner. If a threat appears at greater range, the shooter can bring his weapon hand up to his lead hand, establishing the classic two-handed shooting stance.

Weapon Retention

Most people trying to defeat a handgun-armed opponent will grab the wrist or try to twist the weapon out of the user's hand. The simplest solution is to have sufficient control of the situation that no one is close enough to do so. Police officers and military personnel are trained not to allow potential hostiles too close, but it is not always possible.

Someone who has grabbed the weapon hand or is reaching for it can be sharply pushed away using the free hand. If the push starts them moving one way, and the weapon user takes a step in the opposite direction, the grab may be dislodged. If the attacker tries to come back for a second go, he can be checked with the lead hand, dissuaded with a sharp command or shot as circumstances dictate.

If a grab has already been established, the key is to break the grip. This usually requires sharply twisting the weapon arm while pushing the opponent away. A hand

Using a Submachine Gun

At short-range (less than 20m/65ft), automatic fire ('spray and pray') from a submachine gun is the most effective method for maximizing the chances of a lethal kill.

At longer ranges (more than 45m/148ft), the more selective semi-automatic fire is more effective.

gripping the wrist is pushed open by rotation of the arm within the grasp, loosening the grip and allowing the arm to be yanked free.

If the grip cannot be instantly broken, alternative options include pushing the opponent away by placing the free hand in his face or throat, or striking him with the free hand. Movements need to be short and violent, ideally causing the opponent to lose his balance and weakening his grip. A steady pull in one direction is easy to counter, but a series of sharp yanks is much more difficult to deal with. The goal is to make the opponent's grip on the weapon or the arm holding it slip or loosen; once this is accomplished then it can be freed.

It is not enough to free the arm, as sufficient space must be made to prevent the grab from being re-established. It may be necessary to twist the weapon around and shoot the person who has grabbed it – any attempt to seize a weapon from its user is a potentially lethal threat and must be treated accordingly.

Under Fire

A common rule for firearms combat is 'take cover, not casualties', but this is not always possible. At close range, the critical factor in surviving a gunfight is often the ability to get an effective shot on target first. Being hit, even if the round is stopped by body armour or the wound is not very serious, will disrupt a shooter's aim and possibly cause him to panic and become defensive.

Shooting accurately under fire is extremely difficult due to stress and the effects of adrenaline. Often, many shots are exchanged with very few hits. Shooters who keep their head and act intelligently have many advantages over those who simply blaze away as fast as their weapon will discharge.

If cover is available and the range is not very short, then using it is wise. As already noted, at very short ranges the time taken to seek cover simply may not be available. In this case the only defence is to attack effectively first. However, if hard cover (anything that will stop a bullet) is available then shooting from behind it has several advantages. Obviously there is the protection afforded by the cover, but the fact that the shooter feels a little safer can be a steadying factor, allowing more deliberate and accurate aim. Cover can also be used to rest a weapon, supporting it to improve accuracy.

Movement and Concealment

Movement makes a shooter hard to hit, as well as reducing his own accuracy. Someone who is moving quickly, unless they are headed directly away from or towards the firer, can be very hard to hit. Concealment (anything that will not stop a bullet but obscures

Shooting from Cover

Any solid object or structure can be used as cover, greatly increasing the soldier's chances of survival in a firefight. This is one factor that makes ambushes truly deadly – if one side is shooting from cover and the other is in the open, the combat can be very one-sided.

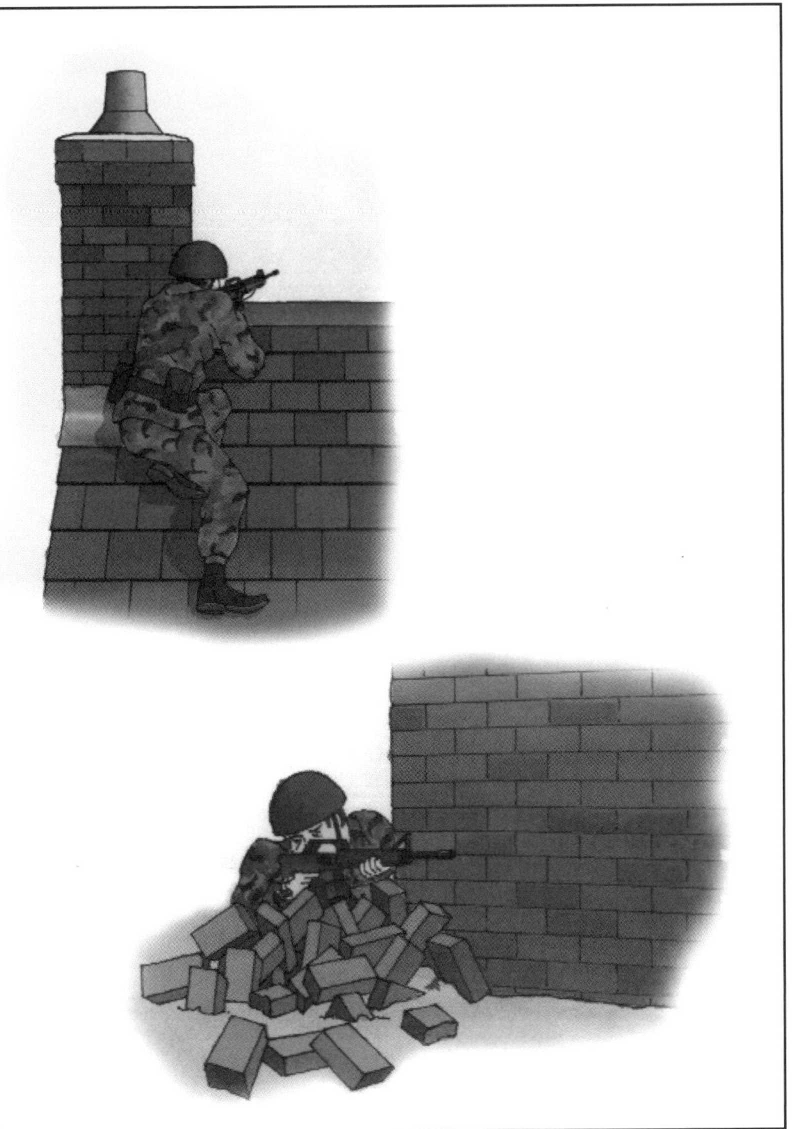

what is beyond it) is highly useful if combined with movement. Even if concealment is not total, hostiles will have trouble targeting someone who can only be partially discerned and is on the move. Total concealment can be used to break contact or to move to a better position.

Movement can also be used to establish a better position, perhaps catching hostiles in a crossfire or moving to a point where their cover is not as effective while maximizing your own. Trained military personnel will use fire-and-movement tactics, whereby some personnel shoot at

Suppressive Fire

Putting a lot of rounds into the general vicinity of the enemy may seem wasteful of ammunition, but the tactical effects are worthwhile as hostiles may be forced to take cover rather than firing.

the enemy while others move to a better position.

Suppressive fire is often used by soldiers caught in a gunfight. This is aimed at the enemy's general position and has the primary goal of driving hostiles into cover or demoralizing them. An enemy gunman who feels that it is too dangerous to stick his head above cover to shoot may slink away or simply stay down. While he is not firing, he is not a threat to troops who are moving around to flank his position or attempting to break contact. If suppressive fire causes enemy casualties then this is a

At long range, harassing fire limits the enemy's freedom of movement even if no casualties are caused.

welcome bonus, but it is primarily a tactical option intended to facilitate an attempt to improve the position of friendlies.

A high volume of fire is also used in counter-ambush drills. The best response to an ambush is to lay down suppressive fire on suspected enemy positions, driving some hostiles under cover and reducing both the accuracy and volume of incoming fire. Friendlies will then react aggressively in many cases, leapfrogging through positions of cover to drive off or defeat the ambushers. Alternatively, it may be possible to advance straight into the ambushers' positions under cover of heavy fire, or to retreat and break contact if the odds are bad.

Close-quarters Battle

When conducting an assault on a building held by hostiles or fighting in urban terrain, combat often takes place at extremely close quarters. Entry into a room is particularly hazardous, as hostiles may be waiting in ambush. Measures to minimize the threat include sudden, surprise assault from several directions and the use of distraction devices such as flashbangs. These, as the name suggests, create a great deal of noise and light that can disorientate or stun anyone within the room. They are unlikely to cause lasting harm but will give anyone entering the area a brief moment to act before the enemy has a chance to respond.

Grenades can also be used to clear a room, but this is not an option if friendlies or non-combatants may be present. Grenades used for this purpose are normally of the fragmentation type, which explode and hurl metal fragments outward.In the movies, grenades send stuntmen flying through the air, but in reality they cause severe puncture wounds and can tear someone in range to pieces. Those not killed or injured may still be stunned by the explosion, but this is very much a secondary effect.

Firepower is the key to winning a close-quarters action of this sort. Troops who are engaged at very close range may resort to bayonets and rifle butts, but for the most part bursts of automatic fire are the solution to most threats. Multiple hits will stop most opponents more or less immediately. Shooting at close range is often from the hip, and victory is often a matter of who gets their weapon on target first.

House-to-house fighting

Personnel engaged in building clearance or house-to-house fighting will work as a team, covering one another and for the most part moving rapidly through the structure. The key is to catch the enemy unprepared, either from an unexpected direction or at a moment where they do not expect attack. Threats are dealt with

Stay Low

Combat troops routinely adopt a low-to-the-ground posture whenever possible; lying or kneeling rather than standing up and making use of banks or dips in the ground. This aids concealment and provides both protection and a stable firing position.

Room Clearing

Clearing a building is a methodical process, with the squad as a whole advancing at the pace rooms are cleared.

Moving past an uncleared room is a serious risk; a proper clearance ensures that no active hostiles remain as a threat.

SAS Squad

Each man in the squad has a role to play and a sector to cover. He concentrates on doing his own job, confident that each of his comrades will deal with whatever contingency arises in his own area of responsibility.

by using overwhelming firepower and extreme aggression, in keeping with the adage that 'the more you use, the less you lose'.

When moving through a building, a handgun may be a better choice than a longarm for the lead member of a team if he has doors to open. A handgun is easier to use at very close range and is more effective one-handed than most rifles or other longarms if the point man must shoot while dealing with doors. Wherever possible, however, shotguns and automatic weapons are the order of the day. Firepower is everything in close-range combat.

Special Forces Tip: Don't...

... point a weapon at anything you are not willing to shoot or otherwise harm.

... put your finger on the trigger unless you intend to shoot.

... forget that a weapon can kill someone by accident, but you are still responsible if you gave it the chance to do so.

FINAL NOTES

Any fight is a tremendously stressful and frightening experience, and once weapons enter the equation the potential for serious injuries increases massively. Many people quail in the face of an armed attack, cowering behind something or just covering their head with their arms and hoping for the best. Occasionally, this is the best possible course of action, but as a rule it is potentially fatal to simply 'fold up' and become passive.

In truth, many 'armed conflict situations' are not really conflicts at all. Often, the possession of weapons by one party causes the other to become passive, and the situation becomes rather different. Where one person is attacking with a weapon and their target is passively covering up or just trying to flee, this is not a conflict. Attempted murder perhaps, but not a fight.

This effect can work for or against us, depending on the situation. A situation where a confrontation begins to escalate and the aggressor produces a knife could get very bad, very quickly. But if the defender draws his sidearm, chances are good that the bad guy will not want to fight any more. If he does, firepower is on the side of the defender. The reverse is also true – if the aggressor is armed and the defender is not, many people will just freeze. If, however, the aggressor's motives are something like robbery or escape from a crime scene, he will probably go on his way without causing much physical harm... but of course this is not guaranteed.

Fighting Back

Tackling a weapon while unarmed or outgunned is a worst-case scenario, but sometimes there is no viable alternative. A person who is attacked with a knife or stick, and who does nothing, will at best be seriously harmed. Fighting back carries many risks, but it does offer a chance of survival. Indeed, no matter how bad things get, if you're still in the fight then you still have a chance. That applies mentally as well as physically. Many people are taken out of the fight mentally by the sight of weapons, when in fact they still have a decent chance to win from a purely physical viewpoint.

If bullets are flying around then staying under cover or at least getting low to the ground is a sensible option, but staying put may or may not be a good choice. Anyone who becomes passive during armed combat surrenders the initiative to the enemy, and can be picked off or taken out at their leisure.

Cool Under Pressure

Properly trained personnel are able to make rational decisions even under extreme pressure. The ability to weigh up a situation and formulate an effective response in a split second can be far more important than any given weapon or item of equipment.

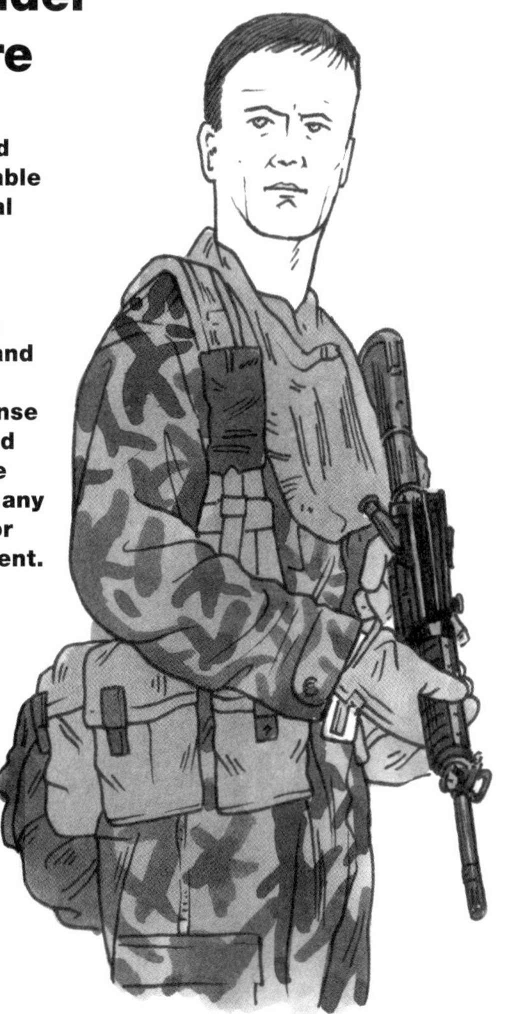

Hitting Back Hard

Military close-quarters combat systems make extensive use of close-range elbow strikes rather than complex martial arts-type blows. Close combat is a quick and dirty business at best, but when the opponent has a weapon in his hand, a rapid put-down is essential.

If others are actively resisting, then the hostiles' attention will be directed at them for the most part, and if they win, then all is well. Likewise, if the hostiles have a mission to accomplish and withdraw after doing so, then anyone who stayed out of the fight should be safe enough. However, friendlies do not always win, and sometimes the enemy's goal is to kill rather than combat being incidental to their mission. In this case, passivity may only delay the inevitable.

Thus taking cover, getting down or hiding should be used actively, as tactics for surviving the situation rather than as a panicked reaction to a situation that has gotten out of control. Wherever possible, the best course of action is to take stock of the situation – numbers and armament of the hostiles, all possible escape routes and likelihood of assistance arriving in time – and to make a plan based on this information.

Planning and Acting

Once the plan is made, it must be carried out with resolution and without hesitation, but not necessarily immediately or in a rushed fashion. Picking the right moment to join a fight or escape from one can make the difference between survival and death. Obviously, if there is a direct attack under way then you have to deal with this, and sometimes it is necessary to make tactical decisions on the fly as one crisis after another unfolds around you. In such a situation, people react according to their training and personality.

The reactions of some people to armed violence may seem incomprehensible to others. Some will actually round on those who came to help them and berate them for being thugs, even during the situation. This sometimes

Rear Stick Up

If the opponent pokes his victim in the back with the weapon, he is telling him where it is. This information can be used to good advantage if the victim decides to turn and sweep the weapon aside. Failure to clear the weapon is likely to be fatal.

happens because a person cannot cope with what is happening and needs to blame someone for their predicament. Since they are frightened and offended by those willing to use violence, they displace their anger onto anyone else who fits that category – even if that person has just risked life and limb on their behalf.

Others will panic or make strange threats about legal action against whoever let this happen (or failed to stop it), or berate their companions for not doing more about it. Again, this is a response to a situation totally beyond that person's control and which they simply cannot cope with.

Fighting Under Pressure

None of these responses is particularly useful, and can hinder attempts by others to deal with the situation. People may also panic or misinterpret what they see, or else try to help in a manner that makes things much worse. One of the drills I use in teaching my own classes is the 'annoying friend drill'. Basically, the student has to deal with a situation while his 'annoying friend' tries to grab him and pull him away.

This drill simulates a scenario where a person is involved in a bad situation and someone with a less clear perception of the circumstances is in the way. As an example, someone who does not want their partner to get involved in a fight might try to grab them and drag them away, immobilizing their limbs just as someone else launches an attack. Or a bystander might see the student reaching for his weapon and think that he is the aggressor, just as the real bad guy starts shooting.

The drill is usually based around something simple, for example, trying to deliver strikes on a focus pad or deploy a weapon while the 'annoying friend', who is apparently oblivious to the real threat, continues to get in the way. It is not acceptable (in the drill at least) to strike or shoot the friend; the student must disentangle himself and deal with the situation despite the well-meaning interference. This drill is mentally and physically challenging, and helps train students to react intelligently under stress in a less than clear-cut situation.

Drills like this one go beyond the purely technical skills of weapon use and force the student to make tactical decisions under extreme pressure, and to use their weapon or unarmed combat skills under whate are distinctly sub-optimal circumstances. Mental preparation of this sort is vital for armed combat because there is no such thing as optimal circumstances.

Acting Fast

Ultimately, the key to wining an armed fight, as in all conflict, is to be willing to take calculated risks and to accept that this situation really is happening to you, and so it must be dealt with. Fear must be put aside in favour of doing what is necessary right now, and you must retain the ability to make intelligent choices as circumstances change. That can mean anything from deciding to break off and escape as things go bad, taking the best opportunity you'll get for an attack, even if it is not ideal, or making a 'no-shoot' decision when the situation requires it.

As already noted, if you're still in the fight then you have a chance to win, so above all you must retain your fighting spirit and willingness to act when the time comes.

Control the Weapon

Controlling the weapon is vital to any defence, but it is only one step on the way. A palm strike to the jaw is an effective knockout blow – and if the user is unconscious then getting control of his weapon becomes fairly straightforward.

Combat Under Pressure

Shooting from good cover at a target in the open is about as ideal a situation as can be hoped for, and accurate shooting is relatively easy.

Once the enemy starts putting suppressing fire into your position, stress mounts and it becomes harder to shoot well. Even simple tasks like changing a magazine can become tricky under the stress of combat. The only answer is endless training that makes these tasks automatic.

GLOSSARY

Arrest and restraint: A body of techniques concerned with the detention of suspects by personnel involved in law-enforcement or security operations. Arrest and restraint (sometimes called control and restraint) techniques are intended to cause as little harm as possible, but may rely on pain compliance to force a suspect into a controllable position.

Blunt force trauma: Some weapons inflict wounding by blunt force, causing bones to break and tissue to tear by the impact of a fast-moving, heavy object with little cutting or piercing capability. Blunt force is particularly dangerous to the head, but is soaked up by any yielding material. Thus a thick leather jacket might be little protection against a knife thrust, but it will mitigate a strike with a stick to some extent. Conversely, some bullet-resistant and stab-resistant body armour will prevent a knife or bullet entering the body but are of little use against a club, kick or the stroke of a rifle butt.

Body armour: Body armour is designed to protect the wearer from various threats. High-end military armour is bulky and heavy, but can stop a rifle bullet from some angles. Lighter armour is effective against lesser threats such as grenade fragments or handgun bullets. There is no such thing as a 'bullet-proof vest' – even the best armour has vulnerable points, but bullet-resistant and knife-resistant armour is available. Some of these vests are light enough to be concealed under clothing but still offer reasonable protection against many threats.

Close assault: Close assault is a military tactic, referring to attacking an enemy force or position by closing to an extremely short distance. High-firepower automatic weapons are favoured for assaults. Hand-to-hand fighting may occur, but where possible the assault is completed by use of firearms and grenades.

Close quarters battle: A military term for combat occurring at short range, usually in close terrain such as a defended position or an urban area. CQB is characterized by high intensity and the possibility of engagement at extremely short range, necessitating weapon-retention and hand-to-hand combat skills.

Entry team: A security, police or military force specializing in entering structures containing armed hostiles. Entry teams may attempt to detain suspects if possible, but are trained to overwhelm any resistance using firepower or perhaps hand-to-hand methods. Entry teams must often operate in very difficult circumstances, such as when trying to rescue hostages held by armed personnel who may not be easily distinguishable from those they are holding.

Firefight: Firefight is a general term applied to situation where two forces exchange gunfire. Firefights are often inconclusive, with a great deal of ammunition expended for relatively few hits. One side will often disengage when its personnel perceive they are not winning.

Fully automatic: A fully-automatic weapon fires and reloads itself from a magazine or belt, and keeps doing it as long as there is ammunition available and the trigger is pressed. Automatic weapons can be wasteful of ammunition but they do permit a target to be sprayed at close range, making them extremely lethal. Some automatic weapons can use 'burst fire' mode instead of full-automatic, which fires a set number of rounds (usually three) for each press of the trigger. Most automatic weapons have a selector that allows semi-automatic and fully automatic capability.

General-purpose machine gun: A general-purpose machine gun, or GPMG, uses heavier-calibre ammunition than an assault rifle and is almost always belt-fed. It will usually have a quick-change barrel so that one barrel can cool while another is being heated by sustained firing. The result is a weapon with somewhat greater range and hitting power than an assault rifle, and much greater sustained firepower. A GPMG is heavier than a light machinegun, and so is its ammunition, so mobility is reduced. For this reason, many militaries include a Light Support Weapon in infantry squads and use the GPMG in a vehicle-mounted role, or from prepared positions.

Grappling: Any situation where the combatants are able to grab hold of one another is a grappling or wrestling situation. Most unarmed fights involve at least some grappling, though skilled fighters learn to use strikes as well as grappling moves when in close combat.

Hand-to-hand: Hand-to-hand combat occurs when combatants are close enough to strike or grapple one another. Firearms may be used at extremely close range, but more often than not it is difficult to shoot against an enemy who is pressing in, or in the midst of a melee where there is a risk of hitting friendlies or non-combatants. Firearms may be used as hand-to-hand weapons by striking with the butt, stabbing with an attached bayonet or blocking an enemy's strike.

Handgun: A handgun is a small firearm intended primarily for use as a *sidearm*. Most police and military personnel use semi-automatic (or self-loading) handguns, which have a large ammunition capacity and are quick to reload using a detachable magazine. Some personnel do use revolvers, which normally carry six rounds in a non-detachable cylinder. Revolvers lack large capacity and are slow to reload, so are not popular except with some police departments and civilian security organizations. Handguns are capable of rapid fire, one shot per pull of the trigger. Although a handgun is normally used in both hands to facilitate accurate shooting, one-handed firing is possible. This allows it to be used at very close quarters, perhaps using the other hand to push an assailant away.

Improvised weapon: Any object that is not intended for use as a weapon, but which is pressed into service as one. Sharp objects can be used to slash and/or stab, and are dealt with using the same techniques as knives. Many blunt objects are analogous to sticks or batons and are defended against in the same way. Heavier blunt instruments tend to be clumsy but can be thrown a short distance or lifted overhead and brought down on the target.

Knife: The knife is perhaps the commonest weapon in the world today. Examples range from custom-made fighting knives and bayonets to kitchen and working knives pressed into service at need. Most knives are designed to primarily either cut or stab, though some can do both equally well. A knife is easy to conceal and requires little training to use. Larger knife-like weapons include machetes, which have heavy blades for chopping through foliage and can be quite large. In some parts of the world a machete is an essential tool and many people carry them routinely, but on the streets of a typical Western city the machete is almost certainly being carried as a weapon.

Knife fighting: There are several styles of knife fighting, but complex knife-versus-knife duels are rather rare. Most knife use is mismatched – i.e. the opponent is unarmed or has an entirely different weapon – and indeed, most 'knife fighters' are actually skilled at killing or injuring someone by surprise rather than using a knife in open combat. Most knife use can better be considered an assassination than 'knife fighting' as such, and in many cases knife techniques are simple and basic.

Light machine guns: Light machine guns are often assigned to the Squad Support Weapon role, essentially providing extra firepower to an infantry squad. These weapons are not much heavier than an assault rifle, but sufficiently so that they may be difficult to use in close combat. They do, however, usually carry a lot of ammunition. Heavier machine guns are more bulky and unlikely to be much use at close quarters, such as if the gun position is assaulted by hostiles.

Longarm: A longarm is any firearm that normally requires both hands to use. Longarms include shotguns, submachine guns, rifles and some light machine guns or squad support weapons. Military and police personnel expecting combat will normally be armed with a longarm of some kind, perhaps backed up with a sidearm, fighting knife, baton and other secondary weapons. Thus both hands are likely to be occupied at the time a close-quarters fight begins, but this is offset by the fact that most longarms make effective hand-to-hand weapons.

Officer safety: A law-enforcement term for a body of technique designed to help officers avoid injury. Some techniques are physical and can also be used for arrest and restraint. Others, such as threat assessment, are non-physical but will shape the officer's response to a situation. Officer safety training usually includes some weapon-retention techniques.

Personal defence weapon: Also known as a PDW, this is, as the name suggests, a defensive weapon. Designs vary but their common feature is to pack a great deal of firepower into a small weapon. Some PDWs are similar to submachine guns and can be considered longarms, though they are small and light compared to an assault rifle. Other designs are not much larger than a typical handgun. PDWs are not intended as 'battlefield' weapons but are generally issued as backup or emergency systems to personnel whose main role is not direct combat with the enemy.

Rifle: Assault rifles are the commonest military longarm. They are light and easy to handle, and can mount a bayonet for close combat. Most assault rifles are fully-automatic weapons; some can use burst-fire mode instead or in addition. Larger-calibre (more powerful) rifles are normally used as sniper weapons and are rarely capable of mounting a bayonet. Most rifles can be used as close combat weapons, striking with the butt.

Semi-automatic: A semi-automatic weapon fires once per pull of the trigger, and reloads itself from an internal or detachable magazine.

Sharp force trauma: Some weapons cause wounding by cutting or piercing the target, causing separation of tissues and significant bleeding. Sharp and pointed weapons need not be moving fast to cause injury – where a club has to be swung, a knife need only be pushed into the target or the blade drawn across flesh. This makes piercing and cutting implements highly dangerous at close quarters and immobilizing them vital in a hand-to-hand fight.

Shotgun: A Shotgun fires a group of pellets or sometimes specialist ammunition such as tear gas rounds. Some combat shotguns are semi-automatic; others are pump-action weapons that require the action to be worked between each shot. Shotguns are also slow to load, but they are useful in many security applications. Thus they are used mainly by law-enforcement personnel and military security teams. A shotgun is usually robust enough to make an excellent close-quarters weapon.

Sidearm: A relatively small, easy-to-carry weapon is termed a sidearm. Historically this includes various types of sword and dagger, but in the modern context it normally refers to a handgun or small submachine gun. Sidearms are normally carried in a shoulder or belt holster and can be relatively easily concealed.

Squad: Military personnel are trained to operate as a team, and as a team of teams of increasing size. The smallest units have different names in various military forces, and may be referred to as fire teams or squads. The main difference between an infantry squad and a similar number of civilians is that the members of a squad are practised at cooperating and will be far more efficient as a group, whereas militia, gunmen or civilians will often act as several individuals with a common aim.

Squad support weapons: A squad support weapon is usually somewhere between a general-purpose machinegun and an assault rifle in size, weight and firepower. Some SSWs are light machineguns, others are based on an assault rifle design and have lesser sustained firepower but can share magazines with the rest of the squad. The role of these weapons is to increase the firepower of an infantry force, and many militaries have a doctrine of always including one in any infantry squad.

Stick fighting: Anyone can pick up a stick and swing it; this requires little skill. However, various styles of stick-fighting do exist and some are quite complex. As a rule, martial arts stick-fighting tends to focus on a stick-vs-stick duel situation, with strikes and parries taking place in what looks a lot like a fencing match. Military and law enforcement stick combat training tends to be simpler, concentrating on the delivery of hard blows, plus a few blocks and perhaps some control and restraint techniques making use of the baton.

Submachine gun: There are two general types of submachinegun. The first is somewhat like a rifle and requires both hands to use effectively. The second is very small, not much bigger than a handgun, and can be carried in a holster as a sidearm. In both cases, submachineguns are capable of semi-automatic or fully-automatic fire, and in some cases burst fire. Submachineguns are light, short and handy, and are effective in close combat. Most are not well suited to being used as a club.

Weapon retention: A body of technique based around keeping control of a weapon in a close-quarters fight. Creating space to use the weapon is an important secondary consideration. Traditionally, weapon-retention skills have been neglected in many quarters, but there is increasing recognition that anyone sent out to do their duty carrying a weapon needs to be trained to retain it and to be able to use it in a close-range and life-threatening situation.

INDEX

Page numbers in *italics* refer to illustrations.